"What a treasure this is! A desperately needed and delightfully accessible introduction to an oft-misunderstood yet essential doctrine. In fact, when it comes to the long haul of Christian living, I can think of no subject more in need of the warm and wide-ranging treatment Luke has given it here. *Sinner Saint* is a resource that will bear much fruit in the lives of all who pick it up. Wish I'd had it myself twenty years ago! Excellent stuff."

—**David Zahl,**
author of *Low Anthropology* and *The Big Relief*

"For anyone who is stuck on the cycle of rededication, backsliding, and shame, this book gives gospel truth to the reality of the Christian life. It reveals a grace that rises up to look sin in the eye. I could not put this book down. Accessible, profound, and deeply needed."

—**Gretchen Ronnevik,**
Author of *Ragged: Spiritual Disciplines*
for the Spiritually Exhausted* and, *Katie Luther:
The Nun Who Escaped to True Freedom

"When a book makes me think deeply about God and sharpens my understanding of Scripture, and does so with gold-standard prose that is clear and lovely, I give that book a standing ovation. When I finished *Sinner Saint: A Surprising Primer to the Christian Life*, I was on my feet. Read. This. Book. Luke Kjolhaug has blessed us all."

"Are you looking for something fun to read that will also bring you closer to Jesus? This wonderful book is for you. It will give you a new perspective on what it means to live as a Christian. And it will set you free."

—Sigurd Grindheim, Ph.D.,
Missionary, The Norwegian Mission Society,
Professor of New Testament, Mekane Yesus Seminary,
Addis Ababa, Ethiopia

"*Sinner Saint* is a wonderfully down-to-earth presentation of Protestants' law-and-gospel heritage. Here we encounter sanctification as growth *in grace*. While Lukas Kjolhaug writes as a Lutheran pastor, Reformed believers like me can be challenged and nourished by his proclamation of core biblical convictions that we share."

—Daniel J. Treier, Ph.D.,
Gunther H. Knoedler Professor of Theology,
Ph.D. Program Director, Wheaton College (IL)

"Is it true that a believer fully redeemed in Christ is a saint but also still a sinner at the same time? In a very honest and engaging manner, Luke Kjolhaug capably establishes biblical and theological grounds for this position while taking the reader on an exploratory journey through the personal and pastoral implications of this dual identity."

—Gaylan Mathiesen, Ph.D.,
Retired Professor of Mission and Evangelism,
Lutheran Brethren Seminary, Fergus Falls (MN)

"Christians are regularly told what do; tragically, they are rarely told who they are. Luke Kjolhaug's new book Sinner Saint very clearly, convincingly, and memorably reminds us of our dual identity, as well as the tremendous importance of embracing this in our everyday lives."

— Nicholas Perrin,
Senior Pastor, Corinth Reformed Church

SINNER SAINT

SINNER SAINT

"A Surprising Primer for the Christian Life"

LUKE KJOLHAUG
Foreword by MICHAEL HORTON

Sinner Saint: A Surprising Primer for the Christian Life
© 2025 New Reformation Publications

All rights reserved. No part of this publication may be reproduced, distributed, or transmitted in any form or by any means, including photocopying, recording, or other electronic or mechanical methods, without the prior written permission of the publisher, except in the case of brief quotations embodied in critical reviews and certain other noncommercial uses permitted by copyright law. For permission requests, write to the publisher at the address below.

Unless otherwise indicated, all Scripture quotations are from The ESV® Bible (The Holy Bible, English Standard Version®), © 2001 by Crossway, a publishing ministry of Good News Publishers. Used by permission. All rights reserved.

Scripture marked (NIV) are quoted from the Holy Bible, New International Version®, NIV®. Copyright © 1973, 1978, 1984, 2011 by Biblica, Inc.™ Used by permission of Zondervan. All rights reserved worldwide. www.zondervan.comThe "NIV" and "New International Version" are trademarks registered in the United States Patent and Trademark Office by Biblica, Inc.™

Published by:
1517 Publishing
PO Box 54032
Irvine, CA 92619-4032

Publisher's Cataloging-in-Publication
(Provided by Cassidy Cataloguing Services, Inc.)

Names: Kjolhaug, Luke, author. | Horton, Michael Scott, writer of foreword.
Title: Sinner saint : a surprising primer for the Christian life / Luke Kjolhaug ; foreword by Michael Horton.
Description: Irvine, CA : 1517 Publishing, [2025] | Includes bibliographical references.
Identifiers: ISBN: 978-1-964419-15-2 (paperback) | 978-1-964419-16-9 (ebook) | 978-1-964419-17-6 (audiobook)
Subjects: LCSH: Christian life. | Sin—Christianity. | God (Christianity)—Righteousness. | God (Christianity)—Love. | BISAC: RELIGION / Christian Living / Spiritual Growth. | RELIGION / Christianity / Lutheran. | RELIGION / Christian Theology / General.
Classification: LCC: BV4501.3 .K46 2025 | DDC: 248.4—dc23

Printed in the United States of America.
Cover art by Zachariah James Stuef.

Contents

Foreword..ix

Chapter 1. Beginnings 1

Chapter 2. Biblical Foundations...15

Chapter 3. Broken Heroes..29

Chapter 4. Law and Gospel.. 43

Chapter 5. Imputation..55

Chapter 6. Common Myths 69

Chapter 7. Responding to Objections.............................. 85

Chapter 8. You're Not Alone 99

Chapter 9. Embracing the Battle 111

Chapter 10. Growing Down 123

Chapter 11. Jesus, Friend of Saints 143

Acknowledgements...147

Foreword

WE'RE ALL LOSERS. WAIT a minute, before you throw this book away just because some gloomy theology nerd said something that offends us all in the well-greased therapeutic Bubble Wrap of late modern societies.

Actually, it's a relief. It's cruel to tell people that they can do anything, be anything, achieve anything. I've never succeeded at space exploration, not out of a lack of interest, but because I suck at math, physics, and other things I'm told are fairly essential. It's good to know our limits, so we can actually discover what we're good at.

But none of us is good at God. That's a relief too, because we know it. Seriously, how many campfires have blazed as you poured out your tears and promised to "make Jesus Lord"? Maybe you have a very different religious background to my upbringing—and the author's—but it's pretty much the same. Even in a totally secular approach—being good without God—the upbeat rhetoric of self-care leaves you wondering, "What's the next rule I have to follow to become a better me?" Learn to forgive yourself, you're wonderful, you're the star of the story you're writing for yourself—blah, blah, blah. It's just more "law" but with a life coach.

There's good news for all of us. Jesus isn't a life coach. He didn't come to give more rules for how to make life work. He didn't come for people who thought they were good, but those who knew they were lost (Luke 5:32). The religious leaders thought they were successful enough at the whole religion game to be able to tell everyone else how to live. But they didn't even follow their own rules, much less those weightier commands God gave for looking out for each other (Mark 7:8-9).

Come on, please join me on your knees as you read this life-changing book: "Lord, be merciful to me a sinner," said the tax-collector. "I tell you," said Jesus, "this man, rather than the Pharisee, went home justified. For everyone who exalts himself will be humbled, but the one who humbles himself will be exalted" (Luke 18:13-14).

Dr. Michael S. Horton

J. Gresham Machen Professor

of Systematic Theology and Apologetics

Westminster Seminary, Escondido, California

CHAPTER 1

Beginnings

I'M ALL ABOUT THE feels. Music especially seems to do it for me. Throw on Faith Hill's "This Kiss" and I'm right back in junior high, building up the courage to ask out my seventh-grade crush. Play anything from Bon Iver's 2011 self-titled album, and I'm transported to the Boundary Waters, windows down, breathing in the pine-scented air as I meet up with an old college roommate for a camping trip. Anberlin's "Dark is the Way, Light is a Place" was the soundtrack to one of the loneliest seasons of my life, so re-listening to any song on that album is sure to strike a minor chord on my heartstrings. I feel, and I tend to feel deeply. One consequence of this personality trait is that my conscience has always been easily troubled. Sensitive might be an even better descriptor.

In elementary school, when I wasn't listening to Faith Hill, I was keeping a running tab of all the bad jokes I had laughed at throughout the day. Each one weighed my heart down a little more heavily. On the bus ride home, I mentally rehearsed the list so that I could confess my failures in detail to my mom. Only then could I expunge my conscience. In my young mind, sanctification in its entirety consisted in not laughing at bad jokes. I should also clarify that by "bad" I don't mean "dirty" in the classic locker-room sense of the term. I'm talking strictly about scatological humor, which was quite popular with the roughneck crowd of rural ragamuffins I ran with. I remember feeling particularly proud of myself one day when I confronted a friend on his heathen joke about an elephant stepping in a cow pie and suggested amending it to an elephant stepping in applesauce. My Christian duty was done. I had saved another soul from perdition. The gospel of our Lord. Thanks be to God.

It's easy to look back and smile at the folly of youth, but at the time, the jokes were no laughing matter. To me, they were deadly serious. Life and death, sin and salvation—the stakes were eternally high. Although I never would have articulated it this way, I was already wrestling with a question that has troubled theologians for millennia: why do believers still struggle with sin? How is it that Christians can continue to wrestle so mightily with something whose power we believe Jesus has destroyed?

As I entered high school, my conscience didn't become any less sensitive. If anything, my growing cognitive faculties exasperated my awareness of my own failings. I once attended a short-term mission trip through Focus on the Family's *Brio* magazine, a publication devoted exclusively to girls. An elite corps of gentlemen were also selected to play the male roles in the evangelistic street drama we performed. One of us played Adam while the other played Jesus. For some reason I was deemed unfit for the role of Jesus, so I channeled all of my original sinner to make my portrayal of the first human being as realistic as possible. I don't think I ever broke character. At one point during the mission trip, a motivational speaker challenged us to get serious in our relationships with God. With sincere conviction in my heart and tears in my eyes I went forward to be prayed over, determined that this would be a turning point in my faith journey. Another time as a teenager I attended an Acquire the Fire youth rally, replete with Christian rock 'n' roll, worship, and messages designed to highlight the challenges posed by the diabolical culture around us. The television series, *Everybody Loves Raymond*, in particular was singled out for its failure to uphold a biblical definition of manhood. By the end of the trip I was convinced I needed to up my sanctification game. This was a regular pattern in my life. Whether it was a speaker at youth group, my pastor's sermon about how "the thought of hell should scare the hell right out of you" (it always did exactly that), or a Bible camp retreat which resulted in new spiritual resolutions, I never missed an opportunity to re-dedicate my life to the Lord. With my sensitive conscience firing on all cylinders, I couldn't quite shake the thought that I was always one misstep away from disappointing God. I recall madly pacing the carpet of my A-frame bedroom after heated arguments with family members, friendship troubles, or moral failings, asking Jesus into my heart again and again for fear that he might have abandoned me because of my sin. Wracked by guilt and shame, I couldn't get past the idea that something must be wrong with me. I felt like a second-class Christian because, at this point in my life, I should have been doing better. I should have been making more progress.

Fast forward to college and young adulthood. The lusts of the flesh struck me in new and exciting ways that I felt powerless to stop. No matter how much I prayed. No matter how many times I re-dedicated my life to the Lord. No matter how much Scripture I read, I still seemed to fall into the same old bad habits. I felt David's words "when I kept silent, my bones wasted away through my groaning all day long" (Ps. 32:3) deep in my heart. In desperation, I called up a long-time mentor of mine, someone I trusted and had turned to in times of crisis, and I spilled the beans. All of them. I vented my struggles, my self-loathing, the overwhelming guilt and shame, the predictable promise to God that things would be different from now on following each relapse. But it was more than simple frustration or anxiety. I was angry. I was angry at myself because of my inability to muster up enough spiritual horsepower to overcome temptation. After all, didn't God say that "no temptation has overtaken you that is not common to man. God is faithful, and he will not let you be tempted beyond your ability, but with the temptation he will also provide the way of escape, that you may be able to endure it" (1 Cor. 10:13)?

I truly believed this verse. But my circumstances and struggles painted a different picture. If God was faithful as the Bible said, the trouble must be with me and my own lack of self-control. And that meant it was up to me to fix it, to slay the giant of sin the way David had Goliath. But progress was slow going. Maybe I wasn't trying hard enough? Maybe my prayers weren't earnest enough? Maybe I wasn't digging deep enough? Maybe I wasn't reading my Bible enough? Maybe I was just a lazy Christian? Maybe I was uniquely heinous? I remember pouring my guts out to this friend, expelling the fire in my bones and blowing it back at him with all the existential fury I could muster: "Shouldn't I be better at this point? Aren't I supposed to be improving as a Christian? Shouldn't sin be less of a problem for me as I grow and mature in Christ? What is wrong with me?!" I was wrestling with the same theological conundrum I had in elementary school: Why is it that Christians still struggle so mightily with sin?

I'm an old man now. Thirty-eight to be exact, the same age as Gandalf in *The Lord of the Rings* (I think). I have lived many lifetimes. The days of youth are long behind me. I'm married with two kids, and I like to think I've grown in wisdom. Yet I've come to discover that marriage and parenthood are less vehicles for personal fulfillment and more crucibles which burn away the dross of my character. And there is a lot of dross. Each day I discover more. Bedtime for the littles seems to be the hour when my Mr. Hyde thinks it's his time to shine. It's the end of the day. I'm exhausted. My wife is exhausted. The kids are exhausted but have no interest in sleep. The stalling tactics start, and with them the shouting matches. It's easy to blame your children, but the hard truth is that my own impatience features prominently in the conflict. Some of my least proud moments as a parent have manifested between the hours of eight and nine PM when everyone is scraping the bottom of the barrel. Last week I expressed my frustration to my gracious wife, who tends to fare a bit better in these moments. I told her, "Shouldn't I be more patient with my kids at this point?! I've had lots of practice, we're on the second kid, so shouldn't we have the ability to respond more calmly to the chaotic ramblings of a four-year-old?!" Again, it's the same theological issue: Why is sin such an ongoing problem in the lives of believers, and what should we do about it?

As a pastor, I have the holy privilege of sitting with people during the best and worst seasons of life. I spend much of my vocation at the extremes of human existence with little time between. It's either a festive celebration (weddings, baptisms, graduations) or a tragedy (funerals, sickness, divorce, addiction). People don't generally call the pastor for water-cooler talk. When I attended seminary, I served part-time as a pastor of visitation. At the time the congregation was quite elderly, so I made a lot of home and hospital visits, praying with parishioners, serving communion, reading Scripture, and talking (mostly listening) about life because they had lived a lot of it and I had much to learn. On one occasion, I was visiting an elderly couple. These were faithful, lifelong Christians who had attended church for years. Both were in their nineties and had recently moved to a memory unit due to the increasing effects of Alzheimer's on the husband. The moment I walked through the door I could tell something was wrong. The husband was in tears. The wife was knitting quietly nearby. I was taken aback, because up until that point I'd known them to be a very cheerful, reserved couple who rarely displayed any negative emotions. "What's wrong?" I asked. It soon came to light that the husband had exchanged harsh words with his wife. He was deeply upset and felt remorseful. The two had been married for fifty-seven years. He expressed to me that he loved his wife deeply, though he knew he had treated her harshly—and he was at a loss. How could this sort of thing happen, he wondered? How could a happily married couple inflict so much pain on one another? With tears streaming down his face, he looked me directly in the eye and said, "Pastor, I know exactly what it is I'm supposed to do. So why the hell don't I do it?!" His words brought to mind those of the Apostle Paul in sharp relief: "For I have the desire to do what is right, but not the ability to carry it out. For I do not do the good I want, but the evil I do not want is what I keep on doing" (Rom.

BEGINNINGS

7:18b-19). He didn't want to hurt his wife. He genuinely loved her and desired to treat her with care. But for him, a lifelong Christian in his nineties, the struggle was real. Again, we're back to the same issue: the ongoing presence of sin in the lives of believers from the cradle to the grave.

What are we to make of this? Why do bad habits and destructive tendencies plague us until our dying day? Why haven't we improved more? Why aren't we farther along in the Christian life? Another way to address this is to speak of the problem of non-transformation or even—as one author so provocatively put it—the problem of Christian mediocrity.[1]

Mediocre Christians

There are all sorts of ways to approach this issue, and each diagnoses the malady differently.

Some claim that Christian mediocrity can always be traced to a lack of willpower. The person simply doesn't want it enough. They're holding back, because when you want something badly enough you will rearrange your life to make it happen. For example, if you want a new truck, you put in the extra hours at work, sacrifice vacation time, work weekends, and do whatever it takes to generate sufficient income to make the purchase. Or, if you want to increase your bench press max, you incrementally add more weight to the bar until you attain your goal. In the same way, if you genuinely want to be a more

---

[1] Robert Markus, *The End of Ancient Christianity* (Cambridge: Cambridge University Press), 1990.

• 7 •

positive, patient, or peaceful human being, you sacrifice and put in the "moral reps" until you've developed stronger spiritual biceps. So, if you encounter a lifelong believer who by all appearances looks spiritually unimpressive, the explanation must be a lack of willpower. They're just bad believers; worse sinners who need an extra dose of God's grace. Some would even describe them as uncommitted Christians who through their own negligence have failed to properly prioritize progress in their spiritual lives.

Others say that, when we encounter non-transformation in someone who claims to be a believer, the only logical explanation must be that they were never a Christian in the first place or (depending on your theological persuasion) that they've lost their faith. Disciples of Jesus should exhibit an upward trending graph in terms of their moral transformation. If consistent progress cannot be seen or measured, if improvement is imperceptible and the struggle with sin continues, this is a clear indicator that no living faith is present. He or she is simply a dead tree lacking the true fruit of sanctification.

The deficiencies of such approaches to sanctification will be explored in greater depth throughout this book. For now, though, let's simply pose the question: what if there was a third option? What if there was another way of approaching the issue, a way of affirming the sin problem in all of its depth and complexity and ugliness—without squinting—yet denying it the power to have the final say? What if our value as human beings could not be exhaustively measured by our own behavior and tendencies and desires, good or bad? What if we could be honest about our foibles and flaws and all of the red-blooded humanity coursing through our

• 8 •

veins and yet boldly claim that God has not rejected us on account of them? What if the Jekyll & Hyde existence were not the exception but the norm? What if ongoing struggle in the life of the believer is not a red flag but rather a sign that the Holy Spirit is powerfully at work?

The Simul

I shared the stories at the beginning of this chapter for one simple reason: to illustrate that the internal civil war occurring in the hearts and minds of believers everywhere, the battle between good and evil, is lifelong. The Christian is sinner, the Christian is saint, and both categories apply simultaneously throughout their lives. We never move past either one. As much as we'd like to imagine that human beings can easily be classified as "good guys" or "bad guys," the reality revealed in Scripture is much more complex, all-encompassing, and devastating. Russian writer Alexandr Solzhenitsyn spent years in the Soviet Gulag system for his political views. During his imprisonment he witnessed and experienced some of the most brutal, inhumane treatment of prisoners imaginable. After his release he wrote about his experiences in *The Gulag Archipelago* where he makes this sweeping statement about human beings:

> If only it were all so simple! If only there were evil people somewhere insidiously committing evil deeds, and it were necessary only to separate them from the rest of us... But the line dividing good and evil cuts through the heart of every human being... At times he is close to being a devil, at times

to sainthood. But his name doesn't change, and to that name we ascribe the whole lot, good and evil.[2]

Solzhenitsyn's observations are thoroughly biblical, giving a modern-day illustration of how deeply "all have sinned and fall short of the glory of God" (Rom. 3:23).

The Christian is a sinner and the Christian is a saint, simultaneously. While this idea has been around throughout much of church history, it wasn't until the time of the Reformation that the teaching was formally codified and explained in a systematic way. The Latin phrase is *simul justus et peccator*, alternately translated as "simultaneously saint and sinner," "simultaneously righteous and sinful," or "at once righteous and sinful." We'll use the word *simul* for short to designate this teaching. The phrase itself comes directly from sixteenth-century reformer Martin Luther, though it was anticipated by predecessors such as Jan Hus over a century earlier, who declared that Christians are "at one and the same time righteous and unrighteous, believing and unbelieving."[3] In his comments on the book of Galatians, Luther defines the *simul* in this seminal statement: "thus a Christian man is righteous and a sinner at the same time, holy and profane, an enemy of God and a child of God." Luther recognizes the seemingly counterintuitive nature of this statement by raising the question himself: "How can these two contradictory things both be

---

[2] Alexandr Solzhenitsyn, *The Gulag Archipelago, 1918-1956: An Experiment in Literary Investigation*, trans. Alexander Solzhenitsyn & Harry Willetts, vol. 1 (New York: Harper & Row Publishers, 1978), 168.

[3] Jan Hus, *Tractatus de ecclesia*, 8; *Johannis Hus Tractatus Responsivus*, ed. Thomson, 27, quoted in Alister McGrath, *Iustitia Dei: A History of the Christian Doctrine of Justification*, 4th ed. (Cambridge: Cambridge University Press, 2020), 202.

• 10 •

true at the same time, that I am a sinner and deserve divine wrath and hate, and that the Father loves me? Here nothing can intervene except Christ the Mediator... A Christian... is loved by the Father, not for his own sake but for the sake of Christ the Beloved."[4]

Two quick clarifications here. First, the *simul* is not a dualistic yin and yang-type situation, where Christians may be (for example) thirty-five percent bad and sixty-five percent good at any given moment, with the forces of good and evil mixed together in an undifferentiated mass. Christians are not partial sinners and partial saints. Instead, they are, at every moment, one hundred percent sinner and one hundred percent saint.[5] We are always completely sinful (on account of our deeds) and completely righteous (on account of Jesus). Now, if you are of the left-brained, mathematician-variety, your head probably hurts. I feel your pain. I used to be an engineer myself, and the numbers just don't add up. We'll get into this more as the book goes on. For now, though, you may want to put your calculator away.

Second, this sinner-saint paradigm does not imply that everything humans do is totally and utterly debauched, perverted, and degenerate. Affirming the presence of an "inner sinner" does not automatically negate the possibility of good. Instead, when we say

---

[4] Martin Luther, *Lectures on Galatians* (1531/5), in *Luther's Works*, American Edition, eds. Jaroslav Pelikan, Helmut T. Lehmann, and Christopher Boyd Brown (St. Louis and Philadelphia: Concordia and Fortress, 1955), 12:232, 235.

[5] According to Alister McGrath, this theological development is uniquely reformational. Prior to Luther, many theologians tended to follow Augustine's description of Christians as *partly* righteous and *partly* sinful (ex quod partim justus, ex quadan partim peculator). In contrast, Luther, at least later in life, saw them as *totally* righteous and *totally* sinful. See *Iustitia Dei: A History of the Christian Doctrine of Justification*, 4th ed. (Cambridge: Cambridge University Press, 2020), 205.

that the category "sinner" never ceases to apply to Christians, what we mean is that every molecule of us is still subject to sin's pull, including our thoughts, words, and deeds. Like a child who has just polished off a bag of Cheetos and goes to play on the furniture, we leave our greasy, sin-stained fingerprints on everything we touch. The prophet Isaiah goes so far as to say that "... All our righteous deeds are like a polluted garment" (Isa. 64:6). In other words, even when I do something good like washing the dishes, I am not doing so for purely altruistic reasons. Part of me is doing it for the selfish desire of human praise; I want a pat on the back from my wife. I want to be recognized for the good I am doing, like the Pharisees Jesus spoke of (see Luke 18:9-14).

The *simul* is a mind-boggler; a category-scrambler with few earthly parallels. After all, you can't be *simul* a good and bad employee. You can't be *simul* an adulterer and a faithful spouse. You can't be *simul* an arsonist and a law-abiding citizen. And despite the antics of Brett Favre, you can't be *simul* a Vikings fan and Packers fan—after all, God spits the lukewarm out of his mouth (Rev. 3:16).

For now, however, we'll simply note that the *simul* forms the foundation for our response to the question of ongoing sin in the life of the believer. We'll discover that this teaching, while not always logical, is unswervingly biblical. It has enormous explanatory power not just scripturally but experientially. In other words, you don't have to be a Christian to appreciate how accurately it describes human behavior. In short, Christians are simultaneously saint and sinner. We are totally sinful and totally righteous at the same time. Yet none of this prevents God from loving us unconditionally and transforming us through his Spirit.

BEGINNINGS

Road Map

Here's where we're headed.

In Chapter 2, we'll talk about the biblical foundations for the teaching of the *simul*, looking specifically at Paul's "divided man" in Romans 7 and also at the war between the flesh and spirit in Galatians 5, among others. Historically, these have been the texts that most-heavily influenced the development of this teaching.

In Chapter 3, we'll take a look at some of the great heroes of the faith and see how sanctification worked out practically in their lives. Through their ongoing struggles and victories, we can describe them as heroes only if we add the descriptor "broken" to them. Moses, David, and Abraham were sinner-saints too, saved not by good works but by faith alone.

In Chapter 4, we'll dive into the intersection between law & gospel and the *simul*. Why was the law given? What is its purpose? And what is the good news?

Chapter 5 deals with the ten-dollar theological term imputation, which is central to our understanding of Christians as sinner-saints. Does God—in Christ—see us according to traits we intrinsically possess or is there an alternate framework he uses? (HINT: It's the second one!)

Chapter 6 goes after some common myths that often arise in discussions surrounding sanctification, including that the greatest barrier to sanctification is bad deeds, sanctification is a two-way street, sanctification is measurable, and sanctification is the reform of our sin nature.

• 13 •

In Chapter 7, we'll respond to the most common objections, including: Doesn't the *simul* create lazy, couch-potato Christians? Isn't the idea that Christians are one hundred percent sinner *and* one hundred saint contrary to fact? It's too fatalistic!

Chapter 8 makes a positive case for the empathic value in affirming a sinner-saint paradigm. When we see others as fellow sufferers susceptible to the trap of sin and equally in need of grace, a whole world of compassion is unlocked.

In Chapter 9, we learn to embrace the internal battle of the saint-sinner as a sign of life rather than a signal that something has gone wrong.

Finally, Chapter 10 presents a fresh vision for what growth (i.e. sanctification) might look like. Most growth paradigms for the Christian life speak of upward independence, but downward dependence is a more helpful descriptor for Christian sanctification.

While this book is apologetic in the sense that it argues for and defends a particular understanding of human nature, I write with a pastoral heart. Moral posturing is an exhausting endeavor and, ultimately, a convenient fiction. But if we are willing to perform an honest self-appraisal and call a thing what it is, we'll re-discover the liberating truth that, in spite of our brokenness, God calls us his beloved sons and daughters. In short, we are sinner and saint, simultaneously.

CHAPTER 2

Biblical Foundations

IN THE 1955 MUSICAL FILM, *Oklahoma!*, a fierce rivalry is brewing between the farmers and the ranchers. At a local social function, the two rival factions collide in a 1900's-era Laura Ingalls Wilder-style dance battle. At the peak of the kerfuffle when they're getting ready to throw down, an elderly widow named Aunt Eller grabs a pistol and fires it wildly into the air, seizing the attention of the crowd. She proceeds to give a speech (via song), and there is a timeless quality to her words which far transcends the frontier justice and dancing cowboys of their original context. Here's what she says: "I'd like to teach you all a little sayin', and learn the words by heart the way you should: I don't say I'm no better than anybody else... but I'll be [danged] if I ain't jist as good!" Her speech typifies the perennial human tendency to measure our value based on where we stand relative to others. Whether you're a nineteenth-century rancher or a famous Instagram influencer in 2023, the default attitude of the human heart hasn't changed much: "I don't say I'm no better than anybody else, but I'll be [danged] if I ain't just as good!" In other words, nobody's perfect, but I'm certainly a little closer to perfect than *that guy* over there. Or, to put it in theological terms, I may not be a total saint, but at least my inner sinner is less annoying than my neighbor's.

But is it true? Is Aunt Eller right? Or is the idea of sinner-saint (Christians as simultaneously sinful and redeemed by God) a more biblically defensible explanation? In other words, what does Scripture have to say about this subject? That's the first load-bearing stone that must be laid as the foundation of the *simul*. To do this, we'll examine a number of passages, beginning with Romans 7.

Romans 7: The Divided Man

In chapter 7 of Romans, the Apostle Paul is having a wrestling match with himself, and he's losing. You can practically feel his frustration and angst oozing off the page as he alternates between smacking his head against the wall and rattling off another line of this (in) famous chapter. At this particular juncture in his masterful epistle, Paul is at pains to describe the relationship between sin, death, and the law. The short answer is this: It's complicated! Even Paul has trouble wrapping his mind around it:

> For I do not understand my own actions. For I do not do what I want, but I do the very thing I hate. Now if I do what I do not want, I agree with the law, that it is good. So now it is no longer I who do it, but sin that dwells within me. For I know that nothing good dwells in me, that is, in my flesh. For I have the desire to do what is right, but not the ability to carry it out. For I do not do the good I want, but the evil I do not want is what I keep on doing. Now if I do what I do not want, it is no longer I who do it, but sin that

BIBLICAL FOUNDATIONS

dwells within me. So I find it to be a law that when I want to do right, evil lies close at hand. For I delight in the law of God, in my inner being, but I see in my members another law waging war against the law of my mind and making me captive to the law of sin that dwells in my members. Wretched man that I am! Who will deliver me from this body of death? Thanks be to God through Jesus Christ our Lord! So then, I myself serve the law of God with my mind, but with my flesh I serve the law of sin (Rom. 7:15-25).

If that sounds like a tongue-twister, you are not the first to think so. Paul argues like a good lawyer, and his arguments are nothing if not sophisticated (and confusing!). But what is he ultimately driving at? Paul is saying that he wants to do good. He, a Christian, genuinely, truly, and sincerely wants to obey God's law, which Jesus summed up in the twin commandments of "Love the Lord your God with all your heart and with all your soul and with all your mind," and "Love your neighbor as yourself" (Matt. 22:37-39). As a disciple of Jesus seeking to imitate his master, this is precisely what Paul wants to do, knows he should do, and is striving to do; love God, love his neighbor. But he keeps hitting a brick wall: He finds himself doing the very things he knows he shouldn't!

It's not that he couldn't differentiate right from wrong. Paul was a Pharisee of Pharisees: he knew the law frontwards and backwards. Knowledge wasn't the problem (Phil. 3:5, Acts 23:6). He knows the right thing to do. The issue is that he knows the right thing to do and yet finds himself doing the wrong thing anyway. In his inner being he delights in God's law, yet in his members, he sees another law waging war. This is fierce battle imagery. There's a war going on,

• 17 •

and the battleground is his heart. His "inner being" (Paul's term for his new nature in Christ) is pulling one way and his "flesh" (Paul's term for his old nature) is pulling another way. He is caught between them, and despite all of his great learning, Paul can't penetrate the paradox that is himself. Two seemingly contradictory realities are simultaneously true: 1. He delights in God. 2. He serves the law of sin. Go figure. But he's not proud of it. The tenor of this passage is not one of pride but deep lament. In verse 24, he makes this broad-sweeping conclusion that rivals the Psalms in its depth of feeling: "Oh wretched man that I am! Who will deliver me from this body of death!" It's hard not to think of Psalm 10:1 here: "Why, O Lord, do you stand far away? Why do you hide yourself in times of trouble?"

One brief interpretive note may be in order here. I take it as a given that the "I" of Romans 7 is the post-converted Paul. Sufficient ink has been spilled over this debate, but the most straightforward reading of the text leads me to believe that, rather than switching perspectives mid-chapter without warning and assuming his listeners will be able to follow along, Paul is here speaking from a Christian point of view.[1]

Such a reading boils down to this: Paul is a divided man, a two-faced Harvey Dent, Jekyll & Hyde character. He finds himself split, violently torn between the desires of his old sin nature and

---

[1] There is neither time nor space to fully examine the details here. Throughout its history of interpretation, commentators have sought to identify the "I" of Romans 7 variously as Adam (e.g. Ernst Kasemann), Israel (e.g. Douglas Moo), the pre-converted Paul (e.g. Augustine), and a kind of transhistorical figure of speech referring to "no one or everyone" (e.g. Kümmel & Bultmann). This is, of course, an over-simplified version of the argument. For a thorough treatment of the issue see Michael Middendorf, *The "I" in the Storm: A Study of Romans 7* (St. Louis: Concordia Publishing), 1997.

BIBLICAL FOUNDATIONS

his new nature. This constant, internal tug-of-war is tearing Paul apart at the seams, and by the end he essentially throws up his hands and says: "Look, I don't understand it. But not only that; I'm also powerless to stop it!" At first glance this might sound defeatist, like he's throwing in the towel. But in the very next verse we discover that nothing could be further from the truth. Instead, Paul continues: "Thanks be to God through Jesus Christ our Lord! So then I, myself serve the law of God with my mind, but with myself I serve the law of sin" (Rom. 7:25). At this point, Paul turns away from himself and directs his gaze toward his Savior. Paul has spent much of the latter portion of chapter 7 looking in the mirror and performing a ruthless self-examination, naming each of his contradictory desires, unable to reconcile the competing passions in his heart. But now, it's as if he looks upward, outside of himself, and remembers the face of Jesus for the first time who—up until this point—had been cropped out of the picture.[2] Paul's hope isn't in self-reform. There's no room for bootstraps theology here. He recognizes that his situation is too drastic for simple behavior modification. His only chance of rescue lies not in sweat equity but in the finished work of Christ, received by faith. When Paul looks inward, he can only see the problem. But when he looks outward and upward, he sees the solution. Like Peter sinking into the Sea of Galilee, when the waves of Paul's own sin and failure overwhelm him because he has lost sight of Jesus, his Savior reaches down and grasps hold of him.

---

[2] This language of "cropping God out of the picture" is adopted from Bob Kellemen, *Counseling Under the Cross: How Martin Luther Applied the Gospel to Daily* Life (Greensboro, NC: New Growth Press), 2017.

Paul refuses to surrender to sin, but he also refuses to gloss over it. Instead, he looks the sin problem clear in the eye and names it for what it is: Yes, I am a divided man. Yes, I am guilty. Yes, I still find myself doing the very things I don't want to do. Yes, I still struggle. I still wrestle. I am far from perfect. But ultimately sin will not win because Christ delivers me from myself!

Galatians 5: Flesh vs. Spirit

In the book of Galatians, we find Paul at his polemical prime. He comes out of the gate swinging, and for good reason: The gospel is on the line. In his other epistles, Paul's tone ranges from that of encouraging uncle to proud parent to weeping brother. But here he is an apologist extraordinaire. There's no time for small talk or niceties or even a standard greeting. Instead, it's right down to business. The "foolish Galatians" (Gal. 3:1a) have been "bewitched" (Gal. 3:1b), and he is "astonished that they are so quickly deserting him who called you in the grace of Christ and are turning to a different Gospel" (Gal. 1:6). False teachers have infiltrated the congregation "to spy out our freedom that we have in Christ Jesus" (Gal. 2:4). These false teachers insist that works of the law (especially circumcision) must be added to faith in Christ if the Galatians hope to secure salvation. Faith may have been enough to *get* them in, but it certainly was not enough to *keep* them in. For that, works were needed. Paul takes these false teachers to task, doubling down on the all-sufficiency of Christ's saving work.

In the latter half of chapter 5, Paul is speaking about the proper use of Christian freedom. In contrast to those who live under the

BIBLICAL FOUNDATIONS

burden of the law, Christians live in freedom, because it is for freedom that Christ has set us free (Gal. 5:1). We are called to use this freedom to "love our neighbors," not "as an opportunity for the flesh" (Gal. 5:13). Rather, we must walk in the Spirit. On the heels of this, Paul introduces some sinner-saint language that is particularly salient for our discussion:

> But I say, walk by the Spirit, and you will not gratify the desires of the flesh. *For the desires of the flesh are against the Spirit, and the desires of the Spirit are against the flesh, for these are opposed to each other, to keep you from doing the things you want to do.* But if you are led by the Spirit, you are not under the law. Now the works of the flesh are evident: sexual immorality, impurity, sensuality, idolatry, sorcery, enmity, strife, jealousy, fits of anger, rivalries, dissensions, divisions, envy, drunkenness, orgies, and things like these. I warn you, as I warned you before, that those who do such things will not inherit the kingdom of God. But the fruit of the Spirit is love, joy, peace, patience, kindness, goodness, faithfulness, gentleness, self-control; against such things there is no law. And those who belong to Christ Jesus have crucified the flesh with its passions and desires. If we live by the Spirit, let us also keep in step with the Spirit. Let us not become conceited, provoking one another, envying one another (Gal. 5:16-26, emphasis mine).

Paul is describing the same internal tug-of-war that he does in Romans 7. The works of the flesh and the Spirit are opposed to keep us from doing the things we want to do. The battle rages on between the new and the old, the forces of good and the forces of evil

• 21 •

doing battle in the hearts of believers. Galatians 5 is different from Romans 7 in that there is no serious interpretive debate over whether Paul is speaking from a pre-conversion perspective (in which case we could dismiss this description as applying only to non-believers). The sinner-saint rivalry, he says, is an ongoing reality for believers. To be sure, it is a decided battle. The outcome is not up for debate, as the works of the flesh are no match for the fruit of the Spirit. The tone of Galatians 5 differs markedly from that of Romans 7. Here, in place of self-despair we find encouragement and exhortation. Since it is for freedom that Christ has set us free (Gal. 5:1), Christians are called to use that freedom not to indulge the flesh but to humbly serve one another in love (Gal. 5:13). This "freedom" Paul speaks of is key. If we belong to Christ, the reality is that all of those evil desires, thoughts, and actions... all of those things that we do and then kick ourselves the moment after... all of the internet histories we can't purge and the words we can't take back and the metaphorical (or literal) knives we've thrown and the wounds we can't heal... all of them were crucified with Christ (v. 24). They died with him on the Cross two thousand years ago at Golgotha. We belong to Jesus. That is the post-Resurrection reality of who we are and whose we are. It is our new identity. And believers must now learn to live and breathe as if that new reality were actually true, walking by the Spirit and not the flesh. Again, the theology of sinner-saint is dominant.

Other Passages

While it is fair to say that Romans 7 and Galatians 5 form the foundation for our understanding of Christians as sinner-saints

BIBLICAL FOUNDATIONS

(*simul*)—redeemed and declared righteous through faith in Christ yet still wrestling against the power of sin—the rest of the New Testament provides additional witness. Here is a brief (though by no means exhaustive) survey:

- In 1 Timothy 1:15, Paul describes himself as "the foremost of sinners." Again, this is the Christian Paul speaking, affirming the existence of his own sin nature (it is present tense; He IS the chief of sinners, not WAS the chief of sinners) while at the same time describing the wonderful reason he can make such an affirmation without caveats: "But I received mercy for this reason, that in me, as the foremost, Jesus Christ might display his perfect patience as an example to those who were to believe in him for eternal life" (1 Tim. 1:16).
- Romans 6:12-13 speaks of the sin that continually seeks to reign or rule in us. Sin wants to set up its throne in our hearts and claim the territory for its own by enticing us to obey its passions. Christians are encouraged to fight against this impulse: "... do not present your members to sin as instruments for unrighteousness but present yourselves to God as those who have been brought from death to life, and your members to God as instruments for righteousness. For sin will have no dominion over you, since you are not under law but under grace" (Rom. 6:13b-14). Why would Paul marshal Christians to spiritual combat if there was no longer any such battle? Sin tries to conscript us into its army, but Christians are to fight tooth and nail against such mastery, since we are no longer slaves to sin but to righteousness (Rom. 6:18).

• 23 •

- Ephesians 4:22 instructs us to "put off your old self, which belongs to your former manner of life and is corrupt through deceitful desires, and to be renewed in the spirit of your minds, and to put on the new self, created after the likeness of God in true righteousness and holiness." Such a command presupposes the presence of a strong old Adam (i.e. sin nature) for the Christian to war against.
- 1 John 1:8-10 gives us this warning: "If we say we have no sin, we deceive ourselves, and the truth is not in us. If we confess our sins, he is faithful and just to forgive us our sins and to cleanse us from all unrighteousness. If we say we have not sinned, we make him a liar, and his word is not in us." John's call to come into the light (i.e. repentance) is predicated on the assumption that sin is happening in the life of the believer; confession cannot occur if there is no sin to confess. Fellowship with Jesus necessarily entails a deep level of self-awareness when it comes to our failures. In the battle with sin, we are called to honesty rather than perfection, because the more honest we are the more keenly we see our need for grace.
- Other related passages include 1 Corinthians 9:27, 2 Corinthians 4:7-11, Philippians 3:21, & Colossians 3:5.

At this point, an astute reader might be picking up on a trend. This list of passages leans heavily on the Apostle Paul. It makes sense that *simul* language springs primarily from a Pauline context. Paul's purpose, after all, is to describe the significance of Jesus' death and Resurrection in hindsight, exploring the ways it impacts what we believe and how we live. It might be said that his language is doctrinal insofar as it seeks to give a cohesive, systematic description of the

BIBLICAL FOUNDATIONS

Christian faith. But what about the Gospels? What about what Jesus had to say? Acknowledging the emphasis on *simul* language within Paul does not imply that the theme is any less central to the Gospels. In the first four books of the New Testament, the idea is simply latent rather than overt. The Gospels are primarily narrative in form rather than didactic. A good story shows rather than tells. The Gospel writers *show* us what Jesus said and did, while Paul *tells* us why and how what Jesus did matters. In short, the people and places and events described by the Gospel writers also reveal the sinner-saint paradigm as normative for the Christian. Here is a sampling of that paradigm:

- Jesus' Sermon on the Mount (Matthew chapters 5-7) "ratchets up" the requirements of the law to reveal the unrighteousness of his listeners; especially those who thought they were particularly righteous (i.e. good) and had drawn this conclusion by relaxing the law (Matt. 5:19). He "ratchets up" not by adding to the law of Moses, but by showing the true depths of the law as it was first revealed in the Old Testament which they had conveniently ignored. It turns out that the law is much more difficult to fulfill than either the Pharisees, Sadducees, or we would like to believe. Jesus diagnoses the problem as being deeper than surface-level. Our sin problem always begins as a heart issue, and the human heart is notorious in its efforts to defend our innocence. He reveals the all-too-human tendency to soft-pedal sins like anger, lust, & divorce, showing that our old nature is still contending for our affections.
- Jesus continually fights against the problem of unbelief and hardness of heart in his disciples (Matt. 17:20, Mark 8:21, Mark 16:11, John 20:24-29, etc.). This pattern persists not

just after the twelve become followers of Christ but even after the Resurrection. Jesus knew that his rag-tag band of fishermen were sinner-saints, one and all. In fact, sometimes their perverse desires were downright demonic. At one point, Jesus went so far as to call Peter out as a devil: "Get behind me, Satan! You are a hindrance to me. For you are not setting your mind on the things of God, but on the things of man" (Matt. 16:23). Even after this rebuke, Peter denied Jesus not once or twice, but three times. The disciples were a motley crew who struggled, doubted, failed, questioned, worried, feared, argued, repented, and wrestled mightily with their own weaknesses.

- Jesus' parable of the Pharisee and tax collector (Luke 18:9-14) reveals the disconnect between a religious person's outward actions and their internal spiritual state. The Pharisee did all of the right stuff. He lived an upstanding moral life. He fasted twice a week. He gave his tithes. He never farted during synagogue (let's just assume). And yet it was the repentant, scum-of-the-earth tax collector (tax collectors were some of the most despised characters of the time) who went home justified. The lesson is clear: We're not as good as we think we are. In fact, it gets worse: Confidence in our own goodness is actually the greatest threat to our relationship with God. Jesus' parable only applies to those who experience such tension between their old and new natures. More on this in Chapter 6.

Sinners Made Saints

Whether it is the words of Moses or Paul or John or Jesus, Scripture paints an unflinchingly honest yet astoundingly hopeful vision of

God's people. We are sinners because we continue to fail and daily need repentance and forgiveness. As a great theologian once put it, "The saints are just the sinners who fall down and get up."[3] Yet the more unbelievable and greater truth is that we are saints by virtue of Jesus, cleansed and redeemed by his holy and precious blood and declared righteous. We may see the sinner, but God only sees the saint. Through faith, we have been clothed in Christ (Gal. 3:26), and not even our worst sins can penetrate his indestructible suit of righteousness.

All Christians acknowledge their struggle with sin. Every believer admits they are imperfect. Such a claim is nothing new nor is it particularly brave. In fact, it has broad consensus among the historic Christian traditions. The disagreement arises when we start talking about how and to what extent this sin still clings to us throughout life. What the *simul* offers is clarification and honesty. It clarifies, because it insists that we are at one and the same time fully (not partially) righteous and fully (not partially) sinful; one hundred percent of each (more on this mathematical paradox in Chapter 7). And it is honest because it fearlessly faces the law in all of its Mount Sinai glory while unashamedly grasping Christ as the sole source of our righteousness. Viewed in such a light, any measuring stick we might use to compare our goodness to others loses all of its force, since God doesn't grade on a curve.

Aunt Eller was wrong. "I don't say I'm no better than anybody else, but I'll be [danged] if I ain't jist as good" is neither a true nor helpful philosophy to live by. Rather, in light of our mutual failure to

---

[3] Bob Carlisle, "We Fall Down," track 1 on *Stories of the Heart*, Benson Records, 1998, compact disc.

hit God's mark, the Christian is pulled ever deeper into the finished nature of Jesus' life and work on our behalf. In our weakness, we have the chance to experience the strength of our Lord more intimately. Sanctification is not fundamentally about our sins slowly being chipped away at as we progress toward personal holiness and ultimately perfection. It is instead a daily exercise in dying to ourselves, where our gaze is continually redirected from the accusing power of our sin and toward the sufficiency of our Savior, who sanctifies us by the Holy Spirit's power.

Yet perhaps an even more convincing apologetic argument for the *simul* would be to see how it plays out in the actual lives of God's people. In the next chapter, we'll look at a few of the great heroes of the faith, to discover how God chose and used them not *because of* their intrinsic goodness, but *despite* their lack of it.

CHAPTER 3

Broken Heroes

EVERYONE LOVES A GOOD hero story. "The Hero's Journey," popularized by Joseph Campbell in his 1949 book, *The Hero With a Thousand Faces*, is an archetypal plot line that every such tale follows. All of the great myths that we read in books and watch on the big screen have a series of stages that the main character follows as he or she develops. Whether it's *The Mandalorian* or *The Hobbit* or *The Sandlot* or *Captain America*, each traces a similar trajectory. "The Hero's Journey" is typically divided up into three main movements:

1. Departure (separation). Think of Frodo leaving the Shire, Bruce Wayne venturing out of Wayne Manor, or Thor departing Asgard.
2. Initiation. This is where conflict with the enemy occurs. The hero is tested and achieves what he or she set out to do, usually at great cost to themselves. Think of Benny "The Jet" Rodriguez in *The Sandlot* jumping over the outfield wall to face his fears and steal the ball from the Beast or Shrek going up against the dragon to rescue Fiona.

3. Return. After the conflict is resolved the character returns home. Often, they are wounded and forever changed, having defeated the enemy and discovered something new about themselves. Think of *The Lion, the Witch, and the Wardrobe* when the Pevensie children return through the wardrobe after their coronation, or Frodo departing Middle Earth for the Grey Havens because his Nazgul knife wound will never fully heal.

In a very real sense, the Bible follows a similar trajectory. If we view Scripture as a single, unified (and *true*) story with one central hero, then every page is about Jesus who left heaven behind to rescue his beloved people, lost and in bondage under the power of sin. In *The Jesus Storybook Bible*, Sally Lloyd-Jones puts it like this:

... people think the Bible is a book of heroes, showing you people you should copy. The Bible does have some heroes in it, but (as you'll soon find out) most of the people in the Bible aren't heroes at all. They make some big mistakes (sometimes on purpose), they get afraid and run away. At times, they're downright mean. No, the Bible isn't a book of heroes. The Bible is most of all a Story. It's an adventure story about a young Hero who comes from a far country to win back his lost treasure. It's a love story about a brave Prince who leaves his palace, his throne—everything—to rescue the ones he loves. It's like the most wonderful of fairy tales that has come true in real life![1]

---

[1] Sally Lloyd-Jones, *The Jesus Storybook Bible* (Grand Rapids: Zondervan, 2007), 15-17.

BROKEN HEROES

It's easy to put our heroes on a pedestal, especially the biblical ones. It's human nature to lionize and even, at times, deify those we admire. The prevalence of sculptures and statues in our world, which functionally immortalize the people we look up to, attests to this. So it's only natural that we approach the pages of Scripture with a similar attitude. We ask questions like, "What is good? What is true? What is beautiful? What is worth imitating about this person? That's where we should focus, right?" And while Scripture is chock full of examples (both good and bad), this tendency to airbrush and romanticize the past actually robs the great heroes of the faith of their humanity and robs God of his power. The truth is that they were flesh and blood, just like you and me. They wrestled. They struggled. They didn't always get it right. Just like us, they were justified not by works but by faith alone.

So, let's look at a few of these broken heroes.

Moses' Anger

Moses had anger issues, and it wasn't just a phase. It was a regular behavioral pattern that he never seemed to fully outgrow. His temper plagued him until his dying day. Let's examine three such outbursts.

In Exodus 2:11-12 we read: "One day, when Moses had grown up, he went out to his people and looked on their burdens, and he saw an Egyptian beating a Hebrew, one of his people. He looked this way and that, and seeing no one, he struck down the Egyptian and hid him in the sand." Let's get this straight: Moses killed an Egyptian. But not only that, he moved the body and sought to cover up his crime. His anger flared up, and he lashed out by committing murder.

• 31 •

SINNER SAINT

Moses, the most humble man who ever lived (Num. 12:13), actually killed someone. He was forty years old when this occurred.

A second story portraying Moses' anger appears in Exodus 32:15-20. At this point, Moses was up on Mount Sinai receiving the Ten Commandments. The Israelites had set up camp at the base of the mountain. Because their leader took so long to return (40 days), they convinced Moses' brother Aaron to make them a golden calf to worship. When Moses finally returned, he was greeted by the sound of singing and dancing. After learning the truth about the people's idolatry, he lost his marbles. Here it is (v. 19):

> And as soon as he came near the camp and saw the calf and the dancing, Moses' anger burned hot, and he threw the tablets out of his hands and broke them at the foot of the mountain. He took the calf that they had made and burned it with fire and ground it to powder and scattered it on the water and made the people of Israel drink it.

That's a pretty strong reaction. You can almost smell the smoke coming out of his ears as he throws down the tablets of stone, Bobby Knight style. The scholarly consensus seems to be that Moses did not actually commit a sin here. His zeal was for the Lord. It was a kind of righteous anger. And yet it's also clear that his emotions got the better of him. God never explicitly told Moses to grind the idol into powder and force the Israelites to drink it. He did that on his own, and as a result of Moses' actions, God had to fashion new tablets. There were repercussions for his flare-up. Moses was about eighty years old when this happened.

• 32 •

BROKEN HEROES

The third account of Moses' rage bubbling over can be found in Numbers 20:2-14. The Israelites were complaining (they did that a lot). There was no water, seemingly for the umpteenth time. They were frustrated and scared, so they did what people tend to do in a crisis: They blamed their leaders, Moses and Aaron. But God came to the rescue. He told Moses and Aaron to speak to a particular rock and promised that when they did, water would flow and their thirst would be quenched. But, again, Moses' temper got the better of him.

Look at Numbers 20:10-12:

> Then Moses and Aaron gathered the assembly together before the rock, and he said to them, "Hear now, you rebels: shall we bring water for you out of this rock?" And Moses lifted up his hand and struck the rock with his staff twice, and water came out abundantly, and the congregation drank, and their livestock. And the Lord said to Moses and Aaron, "Because you did not believe in me, to uphold me as holy in the eyes of the people of Israel, therefore you shall not bring this assembly into the land that I have given them."

Instead of trusting God to fulfill his promise, Moses took the matter into his own hands. He didn't speak to the rock as God had commanded. Instead, he struck it, pridefully belittling the Israelites and speaking harshly to them. He'd had it up to here with these people and their grumbling, and it's hard to blame him. But the consequences of his actions were devastating. God prevented Moses from entering the Promised Land. He and Aaron actually died shortly after this incident, within a stone's throw of the land of Canaan. He was around one hundred and twenty years old at the time.

• 33 •

This is the same Moses whom the author of Hebrews extols, saying that he, "considered the reproach of Christ greater wealth than the treasures of Egypt... [who] left Egypt, not being afraid of the anger of the king, for he endured as seeing him who is invisible" (Heb. 11:26). This is the same Moses who is listed in the faith hall of fame alongside men like Abraham and Noah. Moses, the mighty man of God who led his people out of Egypt, the one who foreshadowed Christ in Deuteronomy 18, the one Numbers 12:13 describes as "a very humble man, more humble than anyone else on the face of the earth."

Moses the brave. Moses the humble. Moses the prophet and leader, yes. But also, Moses the angry. Moses the murderer. Moses the broken. He struggled. He wrestled. Yet God used this broken, forgiven sinner in powerful ways to accomplish his purposes.

Abraham's Fear

The Bible speaks of Abraham as a man of obedience and faith (see Heb. 11:8-19), but in Genesis 12, we see another side of Abraham when he succumbs to his most primal fears.

God had just called Abraham (at this point his name was still Abram) and made a covenant with him (Gen. 12:1-9), promising that he would make him into a great nation, that he would bless him and make his name great, and that all people on earth would be blessed through him. In response, Abraham built an altar and worshiped the Lord. At this point in the story, we might expect a powerful display of trust on Abraham's part or some heroic deed to show his thankfulness. But that's not what we get. Listen to the very next verses, Genesis 12:10-20:

BROKEN HEROES

Now there was a famine in the land. So Abram went down to Egypt to sojourn there, for the famine was severe in the land. When he was about to enter Egypt, he said to Sarai his wife, 'I know that you are a woman beautiful in appearance, and when the Egyptians see you, they will say, "This is his wife." Then they will kill me, but they will let you live. Say you are my sister, that it may go well with me because of you, and that my life may be spared for your sake.' When Abram entered Egypt, the Egyptians saw that the woman was very beautiful. And when the princes of Pharaoh saw her, they praised her to Pharaoh. And the woman was taken into Pharaoh's house. And for her sake he dealt well with Abram; and he had sheep, oxen, male donkeys, male servants, female servants, female donkeys, and camels. But the Lord afflicted Pharaoh and his house with great plagues because of Sarai, Abram's wife. So Pharaoh called Abram and said, 'What is this you have done to me? Why did you not tell me that she was your wife? Why did you say, "She is my sister," so that I took her for my wife? Now then, here is your wife; take her, and go.' And Pharaoh gave men orders concerning him, and they sent him away with his wife and all that he had.

Let's be clear: Abraham didn't just shirk his husbandly duties. He actively used his wife, Sarah, as a shield to save his own skin. He lied about her identity, putting her sexual purity up for bid and allowing her to be taken into a pagan king's harem. His actions reveal his own deep insecurities and fears. Rather than trusting God to preserve his life, Abraham took matters into his own hands. He was looking out for number one, casting others (even those most dear to him) aside

• 35 •

in his quest for security. Ultimately, God was gracious and merciful, rescuing Abraham and Sarah from the hands of the Egyptians instead of punishing them as their sins deserved. God fulfilled his promise by blessing them with Isaac, and through his son Jacob (Israel), God's chosen people would emerge, and the Messiah would eventually arrive. It was not Abraham's saintly behavior but the grace of God that came through in the end. Romans 4:2-5 makes this explicit:

> For if Abraham was justified by works, he has something to boast about, but not before God. For what does the Scripture say? "Abraham believed God, and it was counted to him as righteousness." Now to the one who works, his wages are not counted as a gift but as his due. And to the one who does not work but believes in him who justifies the ungodly, his faith is counted as righteousness.

In short, Abraham was justified not by works but by grace through faith in Christ.

David's Passive Parenting

If King David ever wrote a parenting book, you wouldn't want to buy it.

David's parenting struggles began with an earlier, more infamous sin: his adultery with Bathsheba and subsequent murder of her husband Uriah the Hittite in 2 Samuel 11. God brings the hammer down in the very next chapter, where the prophet Nathan confronts David on his sin. Here it is:

Why have you despised the word of the Lord, to do what is evil in his sight? You have struck down Uriah the Hittite with the sword and have taken his wife to be your wife and have killed him with the sword of the Ammonites. Now therefore the sword shall never depart from your house, because you have despised me and have taken the wife of Uriah the Hittite to be your wife.' Thus says the Lord, 'Behold, I will raise up evil against you out of your own house. And I will take your wives before your eyes and give them to your neighbor, and he shall lie with your wives in the sight of this sun. For you did it secretly, but I will do this thing before all Israel and before the sun.' " David said to Nathan, "I have sinned against the Lord." And Nathan said to David, "The Lord also has put away your sin; you shall not die. Nevertheless, because by this deed you have utterly scorned the Lord, the child who is born to you shall die (2 Sam. 12:9-14).

The fulfillment of this prophecy about David's family unfolds in gory detail throughout the rest of the book. It's tough to read. David's son, Amnon, rapes his virgin half-sister, Tamar. After hearing about this, however, David does absolutely nothing. He refuses to act. Second Samuel 13:21 says that, "When King David heard of all these things, he was very angry." The LXX (the Greek translation of the Hebrew Old Testament most commonly referenced by New Testament authors) adds "But he would not punish his son Amnon, because he loved him, since he was his firstborn." David was playing favorites, and Tamar suffered the consequences. Violated and vulnerable, she found no refuge or protection from her father in her

SINNER SAINT

time of need. Instead, she was forced to turn to her brother Absalom, living in his house as a "desolate woman" (2 Sam. 13:20). She was damaged goods. Women in ancient Israelite society had limited rights to begin with, and in the case of an unmarried, sexually abused young woman, this would have been especially true. Tamar would have been economically dependent upon the generosity of others—likely for the rest of her life—despite the fact that the crime was no fault of her own. David's heartbreaking refusal to stand up for his daughter had devastating long-term consequences.[2]

But this wasn't the last time David failed to act on behalf of his children. The vicious cycle prophesied by Nathan continued. Absalom murdered Amnon to avenge his sister and then fled to Geshur, where he lived for three years. David knew about this, yet again he refused to act: "And the spirit of the king longed to go out to Absalom, because he was comforted about Amnon, since he was dead" (2 Sam. 13:39). Yet his longing for reconciliation didn't translate into action, and for three years, father and son remained estranged. Eventually God intervened, sending "a wise woman from Tekoa" to confront David with a convicting message: "And the woman said, 'Why then have you planned such a thing against the people of God? For in giving this decision the king convicts himself, inasmuch as the king does not bring his banished one home again'" (2 Sam. 14:13). It was only at

---

[2] One commentary explains Tamar's situation in this way: "Because she was no longer a virgin, her worth to her household was diminished, and it is quite possible that no marriage was contracted for her. This is suggested by the comment that she came under the care of Absalom's household rather than David's. She would have lived an unfulfilled existence. The El Amarna texts equate a woman without a husband with an unplowed field" (John H. Walton, Victor H. Matthews, & Mark W. Chavalas, *IVP Old Testament Background Commentary*, Lisle, IL: InterVarsity Press, 2000.)

this point that David finally caved in and commanded that Absalom be returned to him in Jerusalem.

But even after this homecoming, their relationship was still fraught with tension. David wouldn't allow Absalom to live with him, but instead gave him separate living quarters. The estrangement persisted. Eventually, Absalom betrayed David by challenging his father's claim to the throne, forcing David to flee for his life. All-out war ensued until Absalom was finally killed in battle, his hair caught in the branches of a great oak with three javelins thrust through his heart. It's a bitter ending to a tumultuous and heartrending relationship.

As "a man after his [God's] own heart" (1 Sam. 13:14), we might expect some solid James Dobson-style parenting tips from David, but what we get instead is lesson after lesson on how *not* to be a dad. Yet despite his many failures, God used David and his lineage to bring about the birth of Jesus to rescue the world from its sins. One of these messianic titles is actually "Son of David." Clearly, David's righteousness cannot be grounded in his own moral record but in the grace of God, who chose to use him despite his sin. David himself knew this, as the Apostle Paul makes clear when he quotes David's words from Psalm 32 in Romans 4:5-8:

> And to the one who does not work but believes in him who justifies the ungodly, his faith is counted as righteousness, just as David also speaks of the blessing of the one to whom God counts righteousness apart from works: "Blessed are those whose lawless deeds are forgiven, and whose sins are covered; blessed is the man against whom the Lord will not count his sin."

Paul & Barnabas' Split

We often think of Paul and Barnabas as poster boy missionaries; the unstoppable, dynamic missionary duo who boldly proclaimed the gospel in Gentile lands. That is certainly true. What is also true is that they had a bitter disagreement. In fact, it was so bitter that they decided to part ways. Acts 15:36-41 describes the situation which arose as the two prepared for a second missionary journey:

> And after some days Paul said to Barnabas, 'Let us return and visit the brothers in every city where we proclaimed the word of the Lord, and see how they are.' Now Barnabas wanted to take with them John called Mark. But Paul thought best not to take with them one who had withdrawn from them in Pamphylia and had not gone with them to the work. And there arose a sharp disagreement, so that they separated from each other. Barnabas took Mark with him and sailed away to Cyprus, but Paul chose Silas and departed, having been commended by the brothers to the grace of the Lord. And he went through Syria and Cilicia, strengthening the churches.

What was the issue? Why did they split? Barnabas wanted to take his cousin John Mark along to revisit the churches they'd planted on their first missionary journey. But Paul couldn't forget what had happened on that trip. It was still fresh in his memory that Mark had abandoned them in Pamphylia, and Paul didn't want to risk that happening again. In Paul's eyes, Mark had proved himself unreliable, case closed. Barnabas, however, wanted to let bygones be bygones

(Barnabas' namesake means "son of encouragement"). He thought his cousin should get a second chance. Paul and Barnabas couldn't find common ground. The conflict became heated and the two decided to part ways. John Calvin calls it a "melancholy dispute." So, who was right? Who was wrong? We are not told. But the result was that the gospel continued to multiply. Barnabas took John Mark and went to his native Cyprus, while Paul chose Silas and headed to Syria and Cylicia. *Two* missionary teams were sent out rather than just *one*. We don't know for certain how or if Paul and Barnabas' dispute was ever resolved. We know Paul nowhere speaks ill of Barnabas. We know that Paul and John Mark later partnered in ministry. Some scholars suggest that this points toward an eventual reconciliation. In any case, we see once again that God's work is not hindered by human weakness. In 1 Corinthians 15:9-10, Paul makes this shockingly honest statement about the true source of his righteousness:

> For I am the least of the apostles, unworthy to be called an apostle, because I persecuted the church of God. But by the grace of God I am what I am, and his grace toward me was not in vain. On the contrary, I worked harder than any of them, though it was not I, but the grace of God that is with me.

As was the case with Abraham and David and so many others before him, Paul grounds his identity not in his own heroic achievements but in the grace of God. The Lord not only uses Paul in spite of his weakness but actually overcomes his weakness, naming him righteous despite clear evidence to the contrary. He, too, is a sinner-saint; at once righteous and sinful.

Mud Slinging?

It has been said that a key difference between Protestants and Catholics is that "where Catholic teaching tends to stress the sin removed by baptism, and Reformation teaching tends to emphasize the sin remaining after baptism, the excesses of either view needs the corrective of the other."[3] So is this chapter simply another Protestant attempt to fixate on the sin "remaining" versus the sin "removed" in our much-beloved heroes of the faith? Is it mud-slinging, or possibly a smear campaign? I don't think so. At least, that has not been my goal. Instead, the attempt has been made to give a fully-orbed picture of these saints in all their humanity, filled with the same contradictory passions and conflicting impulses present in every human being. When we see them, we see ourselves. A broken hero is the only kind of hero that exists, and that means there is hope for us all.

Moving Forward

In the next chapter we'll examine an important though often overlooked distinction in this whole discussion: the law and the gospel. What are they? Why do they matter? And what do these two little words have to do with our struggle to be better people? As it turns out, a whole lot.

---

[3] Thomas C. Oden, *Classic Christianity* (San Francisco: HarperCollins, 2009), 669.

CHAPTER 4

Law and Gospel

IF YOU'VE SPENT ANY time at all in American churches, it's likely that terms like sin, atonement, guilt, righteousness, justification, glory, being "on fire for the Lord," backsliding, sanctification, and of course the impenetrable "hedge of protection" (apparently Satan has yet to figure out how to permeate a row of shrubbery) are familiar to you. Two such terms we'll focus on in this chapter are "the law" and "the gospel." These words are sometimes bandied about with such liberality that we assume everyone using them shares a common definition. Unfortunately, such is not always the case. This can lead to ambiguity, and the topic therefore requires clarification, particularly as it applies to our discussion of the sinner-saint paradigm.

The Law: When You Give a Toddler a Chainsaw

Let's start with a definition. What is the law? Here is how my catechism defines it: "The law is that teaching of the Word of God which tells me how I am to be and what I am to do and not to do."[1] As we read in Leviticus 19:2b: "Be holy because I, the Lord your God, am holy." The law consists of the "do" words of Scripture. Whenever we encounter a commandment, a "thou shalt" or "thou shalt not," we're hearing the law. The law is a command, typically found in the imperative mood. The ten commandments (Ex. 20:1-17) are a summary of God's law, as are Jesus' words in Matthew 22:37, 39: "You shall love the Lord your God with all your heart and with all your soul and with all your mind"... and "You shall love your neighbor as yourself." Do this. Don't do this. You should be this way. You shouldn't be that way. Obey. Turn right. Turn left. Go west. These kinds of words all fall under the category of law, telling us how we are to be, what we are to do and not to do.

But let's step back and ask a bigger question, one whose answer may seem self-evident: Why was the law given? To what end, and for what purpose? Our knee-jerk response is often something along the lines of "well, to fix the problem, obviously" or "to make things better." Laws are the seawalls we erect to keep the chaotic madness of human passion at bay. The law is our go-to. After all, it's written on the human heart (Rom. 2:15). If someone is doing something they shouldn't, harming themselves or others, the best defense against such behavior is the law. People speed, so we erect speed limit signs. People kill, so we make homicide illegal. People tend to touch the glass, so we make signs that say, "Do not touch glass." Laws, rules, and regulations serve as a deterrent against crime and help curb bad behavior, reminding us to straighten up or face the consequences.

---

[1] *An Explanation of Luther's Small Catechism*, 2nd edition, ed. Warren Olsen and David Rinden (Fergus Falls: *Faith and Fellowship Press*, 1992), 11.

LAW AND GOSPEL

To that end, the law makes for a more stable, just, and less chaotic planet earth, and for that, we must be thankful. God's law is holy and righteous and good (Rom. 7:12), and David extols its virtues when he says, "The law of the Lord is perfect, reviving the soul; the testimony of the Lord is sure, making wise the simple; the precepts of the Lord are right, rejoicing the heart; the commandment of the Lord is pure, enlightening the eyes; the fear of the Lord is clean, enduring forever; the rules of the Lord are true, and righteous altogether" (Ps. 19:7-9).

The law is good and salutary and necessary. But the law also does something unexpected, flipping a switch deep within us. It actually awakens our old Adam. When our sin nature comes in contact with the law, swords are drawn, shots are fired, and an internal revolutionary war is inaugurated. Our old Adam hears the siren song of the law and gains new strength, seeking to overthrow the lordship of Christ and seize the throne of our hearts for himself. The result is that, ironically, the law ends up producing the very thing it seeks to prevent: sin. The Apostle Paul puts it like this:

> What then shall we say? That the law is sin? By no means! Yet if it had not been for the law, I would not have known sin. For I would not have known what it is to covet if the law had not said, 'You shall not covet.' *But sin, seizing an opportunity through the commandment, produced in me all kinds of covetousness. For apart from the law, sin lies dead. I was once alive apart from the law, but when the commandment came, sin came alive and I died. The very commandment that promised life proved to be death to me. For sin, seizing an opportunity through the commandment, deceived me and through it killed me.* So the law is holy, and the commandment is holy and righteous and good. Did

that which is good, then, bring death to me? By no means! It was sin, producing death in me through what is good, in order that sin might be shown to be sin, and through the commandment might become sinful beyond measure. For we know that the law is spiritual, but I am of the flesh, sold under sin (Rom. 7:7-14, emphasis mine).

Look closely. Read it, and then reread it. You'll notice a counter-intuitive relationship between sin and the law at play here. The *good* law becomes conscripted by our *bad* sin nature and used for *bad* purposes. The law is good, but our sin nature puts it to evil use. It's a bit like putting a chainsaw in the hands of a toddler: A good and useful tool all of a sudden becomes deadly, because the toddler will use it for purposes it wasn't designed for. This is how it is with the law: The very commandments which, if we obeyed them fully would lead to life, end up bringing death because they show us how far short we fall.

Here's how this works, practically speaking. You're at Subway, ordering a 12" Cold Cut Combo as God intended. On the other side of the glass are the ingredients that make up this heavenly delight: bread and onions and tomatoes and jalapeños and salami and turkey and ham and pepper jack cheese. And you're enjoying the view, looking down lovingly at all of those precious items. But then you see the sign: "Do not touch glass!" Really, it's the exclamation point that gets you. Up until then, you'd never have thought of touching the glass. But now you do, and you can't stop thinking about it and you find your fingers—almost unconsciously—inching toward the glass. How did this change take place? How did the thought come to you? The

LAW AND GOSPEL

sign itself caused it! The law (don't do this!) activated some primal part of your old Adam, stirring up rebellion and mischief. The sin in you grabbed hold of the law and produced the very sin it was meant to curtail. It's the old "Don't think about pink elephants" experiment. What are you thinking of? Pink elephants, and precisely because you were told not to. The law which promised life proved to be death.

Here's another example. Let's say you've been poor about keeping in touch with your family. Maybe you call your siblings on holidays, but even that is sporadic. From day-to-day, your conscience vacillates between apathy and guilt over this failure of yours. So one day you're talking to your mom over the phone, and she mentions off-handedly that your sister's birthday is coming up. "Great!" you think. "This will give me a reason to call her. It's been way too long," and you actually make plans to follow through. But then your mom continues, "You really should call her, you know. She gets lonely. I know we all have busy lives but it's the least you can do. Even just a ten minute call. Not that I'm trying to guilt you." Now you might start to feel differently, don't you? Now you might start to feel like maybe you won't call your sister after all. What happened? How did that change occur? The law entered the picture. Hearing the good news about the upcoming birthday was sufficient to move you toward positive action, but then came the command: "You *should*" arrived. And with the command, sin came alive. "Well now I don't want to," you think as you hang up the phone.

We are hard-wired to think that the law is the answer to whatever ails us. The apostle Paul calls this justification by works of the law, and it's endemic to the human condition. By nature, the law just makes sense. We understand rules. We understand regulations. We cling to them because they give us the illusion of control. To a certain degree, you don't even have to be a Christian to "get" the law. Romans 2:14-15 says: "For when Gentiles, who do not have the law, by nature do what the law requires, they are a law to themselves, even though they do not have the law. They show that the work of the law is written on their hearts, while their conscience also bears witness, and their conflicting thoughts accuse or even excuse them." In other words, even the basest of pagans has some understanding—however warped—of the law. It is written on every human heart.

Doing more and trying harder is always going to be the solution that makes the most sense to us. The law was given to make things better, or so we assume. But that's not actually what Scripture teaches. Ironically, the opposite is true: The law makes things worse! How so? Romans 5:20-21 says: "Now the law came in to increase the trespass, but where sin increased, grace abounded all the more, so that, as sin reigned in death, grace might also reign through righteousness leading to eternal life through Jesus Christ our Lord." Why did the law come? To decrease the trespass? No, but to increase the trespass. To exacerbate it. Like a giant, 10x magnifying mirror, the law reveals our sinfulness until it expands to fill the entire frame, i.e. "increasing" it. The law doesn't fix the sin problem. It was never meant to. Instead, it drives us to Jesus. St. Augustine puts it like this: "The law is given not to take away sin nor to deliver us from it but to reveal what sin is before grace comes."[2]

Whether it's raising kids, managing people, or pursuing spiritual disciplines, we tend to believe that the law will fix things. If someone isn't behaving the way I want or producing their quota, I just

---

[2] Gerald Bray, *Ancient Christian Commentary on Scripture: Romans,* ed. Thomas C. Oden, 1st ed., vol. 6, 29 vols. (Downers Grove, IL: InterVarsity Press, 1998).169.

LAW AND GOSPEL

need to apply a little more pressure from the law. More commands, more threats, more punishments, and more discipline. But such an approach, especially when applied to our spiritual lives, misunderstands the law's purpose and mistakes the diagnosis for the cure. The law gives us a spiritual CT scan, and the results are dire indeed: "All have sinned and fall short of the glory of God" (Rom. 3:23). The law shows us we are sinful: "... through the law comes knowledge of sin" (Rom. 3:20). But a CT scanner can do nothing to heal you. The treatment for cancer is not more CT scans. For that, medicine is needed. Namely, the gospel.

The Gospel: The Divine Ceasefire

Again, definitions are good. What is the gospel? Here is one helpful response, once more taken from the explanation to the catechism: "The Gospel is the good news in which God tells me what He has done for me through Jesus Christ, especially in dying for my sin and rising in victory over death and Satan."[3] Such a definition springs directly from Scripture:

> Now I would remind you, brothers, of the gospel I preached to you, which you received, in which you stand, and by which you are being saved, if you hold fast to the word I preached to you—unless you believed in vain. For I delivered to you as of first importance what I also received: that Christ died for our sins in accordance with the Scriptures, that he was buried, that he was raised on the third day in accordance

[3] *An Explanation of Luther's Small Catechism*, 11.

• 49 •

with the Scriptures, and that he appeared to Cephas, then to the twelve (1 Cor. 15:1-5).

The word "gospel" is used by Christians in any number of ways to refer to various aspects of the Christian faith. But semantically speaking, the term simply means "good news." When two armies clashed on the battlefield, the winning side would dispatch a runner to bring the news of victory to the king. As the king stood atop the city wall, he would see the cloud of dust rising up from the feet of the runner as he approached from a long way off. The good news of victory delivered by the runner was called "gospel." This is the imagery behind Isaiah 52:7: "How beautiful upon the mountains are the feet of him who brings good news, who publishes peace, who brings good news of happiness, who publishes salvation, who says to Zion, 'Your God reigns.'"

Where the law says "Do," the gospel says "Done." Where the law is a command, the gospel is a promise. Where the law is directed at human effort, the gospel is God's work from beginning to end. Where the law is the diagnostic tool (the spiritual CT scan), the gospel is the cure (the medicine that puts things right and restores health to the body).

The gospel also operates in a very unique way. Imagine someone hearing good news for the first time. Perhaps an elderly couple receives a phone call from their daughter that she is pregnant and they are soon-to-be grandparents. Or imagine soldiers in World War II-era Europe hearing the V-E Day address over the radio, announcing that the war is over. How would the elderly couple and the soldiers respond? We might imagine the new grandparents smiling,

LAW AND GOSPEL

expressing joy and possibly disbelief at their good fortune. Maybe a tear even rolls down grandpa's cheek. In the case of the soldiers, the reaction might be more immediate and primal. There is a chorus of whoops and a volley of celebratory gunshots. Laughter and shouting and dancing and singing. In both cases, the reaction was elicited by the announcement of good news. No further action was required. Imagine how insulting it would have been had the newly christened grandparents responded to the gospel of their grandchild by asking their daughter, "OK. What do you want us to do about it?" Or if the soldiers reacting to the ceasefire had said, "That's wonderful news but what action are we supposed to take?" Such reactions miss the whole point, and in fact turn the gospel into law. The gospel is a gift, pure and simple.

While the law is something we intuitively get, the gospel is not. To one extent or another the law is in our bones. It is the default operating system of every human heart. "Do more." "Try harder." These are words of law, and they are everywhere we look from the gridiron to the gym to the boardroom to Instagram to New Year's resolutions. Law is our native tongue. The gospel, on the other hand—this "done" word—is utterly foreign to us, precisely because it doesn't originate in the human heart but comes from outside ourselves.

The apostle Paul speaks of the scandal of the Cross (1 Cor. 1:17-31), how it is a stumbling block to both Jews and Greeks. To the casual observer, the Cross is the very epitome of foolishness. It appears like defeat, a naked body nailed to a piece of wood. No one in their right mind walking along the Appian Way—the ancient Roman road lined with six thousand crosses of crucified slaves—would point up and say, "Wow, those look like a bunch of winners!"

Yet it is precisely in the apparent foolishness of the Cross that the power of God rests. The Cross is scandalous because it symbolizes weakness, not strength. But it is also scandalous because it is good news for sinners. When Jesus cried out "It is finished" (John 19:30) from the Cross, he wasn't speaking metaphorically. He meant it quite literally. The battle is done! The war is won! The chasm between sinful humanity and a holy God has been breached, once and for all. The head of the serpent was truly crushed and a permanent beachhead against the forces of evil established. Sin was forgiven, and everything necessary for our salvation accomplished. While we spat and mocked and pounded the nails, our Lord suffered and died and fought for our souls: "And Jesus said, 'Father, forgive them, for they know not what they do.' And they cast lots to divide his garments" (Luke 23:34).

The gospel is good news only insofar as it is not about us. To be clear, it certainly matters to us. It affects us. It is for us. But it is not about us. It is about Jesus. The minute the gospel becomes about us rather than Christ, it is no longer good news, since human beings are by definition, at least biblically speaking, *not* good, "... for the intention of man's heart is evil from his youth..." (Gen. 8:21). With the gospel, God does the heavy lifting. More than that, He is the active *DOer* of the verbs while we are the passive recipients. We arrive on the Great Physician's operating table not simply sick or incapacitated but dead:

And you were dead in the trespasses and sins in which you once walked, following the course of this world, following the prince of the power of the air, the spirit that is now at work in the sons of disobedience—among whom we all once lived in the passions of our flesh, carrying out the desires of the body and the mind, and were by nature children of wrath, like the rest of mankind. But God, being rich in mercy, because of the great love with which he loved us, even when we were dead in our trespasses, made us alive together with Christ—by grace you have been saved—and raised us up with him and seated us with him in the heavenly places in Christ Jesus (Eph. 2:1-6).

Salvation is a one-way street. God takes our spiritually dead, lifeless corpses and breathes new life into them, raising us up to the heavenly places in Christ Jesus. This is why the gospel is practically non-translatable to our law-fluent hearts: The unbelievably good news of the gospel is not dependent on doing but believing. It is received, not achieved.

Why It Matters

Why is it so important to distinguish these two ways of speaking: the law and the gospel? And how does it apply to our discussion of sinner-saints and sanctification in the Christian life? The next chapter takes us another step further in that direction. Sanctification is often spoken of as "our part" in our relationship with God. Of course, we'll always pay lip service to the idea that the Holy Spirit is our helper, but when it comes to the nuts and bolts—at least functionally-speaking—we treat ourselves as the subjects of the verbs. In other words, while justification may be "gospel business" in our minds, sanctification is primarily "law business." A proper distinction between law and gospel, however, enables us to rightly understand God as the source of both. And if human beings are to be described as "at once righteous and sinful," the teaching of imputation is the hidden hinge upon which everything turns.

CHAPTER 5

Imputation

ONE OF THE MOST surprising doctrines of the faith is imputation. Most Christians have at least some familiarity with doctrines like creation, predestination, and eschatology. But if you bust out imputation at the youth group open mic night, you're likely to get a sea of puzzled faces staring back at you. Imputation is not common parlance. Also, it doesn't rhyme with anything (though it will net you precisely 42 Scrabble points if you manage to hit a triple word score). But this often-neglected doctrine is nonetheless central to the way God works and therefore crucial for sinner-saints if we hope to honestly self-reflect.

So, let's start with a story:

On May 1, 2009 at the 135th running of the Kentucky Derby a smaller horse named Mine That Bird entered the race at 50-1 odds. Mine That Bird had not fared well in his two previous races. So it was no surprise that the long-shot horse struggled from the start of the race. Mine That Bird and jockey Calvin Borel got squeezed between the other horses and quickly dropped into last place. At the first quarter-mile stage, Mine

That Bird was still running dead last. At one point, he was so far behind the other horses that NBC's announcer Tom Durkin at first missed seeing him. But at the three-eighths pole, Mine That Bird started gaining on the other horses. After passing Atomic Rain, the horse took off. As Borel rode his horse around the eighth pole, he guided Mine That Bird between the rail and another horse. From that point Mine That Bird took off to victory, winning the mile race by 6 and ¾ lengths. The victory stunned the horse racing world. Even Mine That Bird's owner said, "[The victory] wasn't something that was on our radar." Another horse owner said, "I was like, What happened? It was a shocker." But Mine That Bird's jockey, Calvin Borel, wasn't shocked. When asked what happened during the race, Borel simply said, "I rode him like a good horse."[1]

Let's pause here. Borel's account of how he won might not seem all that profound at first blush. "I rode him like a good horse." But dig a little deeper and we'll see imputation at work. What is he actually saying? He's saying that he treated Mine That Bird, who was in last place, as if he were in first place. He viewed and treated a horse that by any objective standard was performing poorly as if he were performing well. He treated a bad horse as if he were good. The jockey ascribed the quality of "goodness" to his horse, despite all evidence to the contrary. In other words, Borel imputed righteousness to Mine That Bird, and the result was a horse set free. The horse's "goodness"

---

[1] Editors of Preaching Today, "Jockey Wins by Imputing Goodness to His Horse," originally published 3/21/13, copyright Preaching Today, https://www.preachingtoday .com/illustrations/2013/march/2032513.html, accessed on 4/7/2024.

IMPUTATION

was not based upon its performance (good or bad) but solely upon the declaration of the rider.

When we impute qualities to something or someone else, we ascribe to them traits that they do not intrinsically possess, and we agree to treat them on the basis of those traits. For example, when I engage my four-year-old daughter in conversation at the dinner table by asking her how her day went, knowing full well that it consisted entirely of naps, Bluey, and Lincoln Logs, I am ascribing the quality of maturity to her. I am viewing and treating her as if she were an adult even though, in point of fact, she is not. When I impute the quality of adulthood to my very un-adult child, the result is deeply transformative and life-giving. She begins to understand her relationship with her father in terms of something other than performance and hierarchy. Her behavior actually changes to mirror the quality ascribed to her, and she becomes who her dad says she is. In other words, she starts to see herself as an adult and begins (sometimes in practically imperceptible ways, to be sure) to act like it.

Another helpful example is that of a newly married couple. When the giggling, blushing bride and groom stand at the altar on their wedding day and make their vows, they don't understand the full implications of what they are promising. And thank God, because if they did, no one would ever get married! They're promising faithfulness unto death. For the next 5, 10, 25, or 50 years, they're promising never to cast a romantic glance or lustful thought at another human being, either in-person or virtually. They're promising to not for one moment emotionally detach from their spouse. They're promising to never pursue an affair of the heart. "For better, for worse, for richer, for poorer, in sickness and in health, to love and to cherish, until death do us part." That's a big ask! Passionate human beings that we are, how can we ever hope to achieve such a level of trustworthiness? And how can we learn to actually trust another member of the human race with our deepest, most intimate selves, knowing that they are just as flawed as we are? There is only one way: Imputation. We must, on some level, impute the quality of faithfulness to them. We must learn to treat our spouse as if they were 100% trustworthy, reliable, and faithful in each and every circumstance during each and every moment of their lives, even though he/she (and we) are human. This is the only way that trust can actually originate and grow in a marriage relationship—when love isn't based upon the moral record of the beloved. The alternative is actually quite horrifying, an image of guilt and shame and loneliness. Sarah Hinlicky Wilson paints the following vivid illustration of such an alternative, and it's worth quoting at length:

> Picture this: a bride and groom dashing out of the church, through the showers of birdseed and into the limo, all aglow with the light of love from the vows they've just taken. In the backseat of the car, en route to the reception, they embrace and kiss. Then the groom announces that he has something to say. "Now you realize, my dear, that, as far as I'm concerned, we can't really say we're married, because I don't know yet what kind of wife you'll turn out to be. I hope for the best, of course. And I'll help you all I can. But only at the end of our lives will I be able to tell if you've lived up to my expectations. If you have—then, and only then, I'll agree that we truly got married today. But if you don't, then as far as I'm concerned we were never married at all. After all, how

can I call you my wife if you fail to be a wife to me?" Under such circumstances, it will not be a happy honeymoon—if there's one at all. A wife cannot be a wife if her whole existence as wife is conditional and under constant scrutiny (likewise for a husband). She will certainly fail. This groom has completely misunderstood [the power of marriage to transform the beloved]. The couple that tied the knot only 60 minutes ago is every bit as married as the couple celebrating their 60th anniversary. Whatever happens in the course of the marriage does not affect the "married-ness" of that couple.[2]

Imputation happens when someone is treated on the basis of qualities that he or she does not inherently possess. Such treatment is the only way to unlock genuine, reciprocal love. In other words, it is only when you believe that your lovability is not conditioned upon your willingness or ability to change that you become willing and able to change. As Shakespeare once said, "Love is not love which alters when it alteration finds" (Sonnet 116). Imputation frees both the lover and beloved from the burden of unmanageable expectations and relational contingencies that would otherwise suffocate them, creating space for mercy and forgiveness to flourish.

---

[2] Sarah Hinlicky Wilson, "What's His Is Ours," Christianity Today, 9-14-12, accessed on 3-7-24, https://www.christianitytoday.com/ct/2012/september/whats-his-is-ours.html. Reprinted here with permission from the author.

Toward a Biblical Understanding

Scripture speaks of this doctrine using synonyms like "reckon," "account," or "credit." Romans 4:3-8 provides a good starting point for our purposes, where the ESV translates the Greek *logizomai as* "count." Watch for this word, which I've highlighted below, because it's all over:

> For what does the Scripture say? "Abraham believed God, and it was **counted** to him as righteousness." Now to the one who works, his wages are not **counted** as a gift but as his due. And to the one who does not work but believes in him who justifies the ungodly, his faith is **counted** as righteousness, just as David also speaks of the blessing of the one to whom God **counts** righteousness apart from works: "Blessed are those whose lawless deeds are forgiven, and whose sins are covered; blessed is the man against whom the Lord will not **count** his sin."

Notice how frequently the term is employed in these few short verses. In his argument for justification by faith alone, Paul is using Abraham and David, possibly the two most heroic figures of the Jewish faith, to bolster his claims. It was not Abraham's deeds that made him righteous before God, though he had no shortage of good deeds. And it was not David's good works that earned God's favor, though he was considered "a man after God's own heart" (1 Sam. 13:14). No. Thousands of years before Christ, *sola fide* was still operative. Justification still happened by faith alone; by believing. God declared (reckoned, accounted) Abraham & David to be righteous,

IMPUTATION

and so they were. As we discovered in Chapter 3, even these great heroes of the faith had a cadre of marks against them: lust, sexual assault, murder, fear, lying, and doubt, just to name a few. Yet somehow their checkered pasts were not enough to prevent God from labeling them "righteous." How can this be true? The only explanation is that such a declaration must hang on something other than their intrinsic goodness.

Imputation has two parts, one of which we are much better acquainted with than the other. The chief passage for understanding this is 2 Corinthians 5:16-21:

> From now on, therefore, we regard no one according to the flesh. Even though we once regarded Christ according to the flesh, we regard him thus no longer. Therefore, if anyone is in Christ, he is a new creation. The old has passed away; behold, the new has come. All this is from God, who through Christ reconciled us to himself and gave us the ministry of reconciliation; that is, in Christ God was reconciling the world to himself, not counting their trespasses against them, and entrusting to us the message of reconciliation. Therefore, we are ambassadors for Christ, God making his appeal through us. We implore you on behalf of Christ, be reconciled to God. *For our sake he made him to be sin who knew no sin, so that in him we might become the righteousness of God* (emphasis mine).

The very last verse (v. 21) is particularly important. Paul is speaking of a great exchange that happens through Christ's reconciling work on the Cross, and there are two parts to this exchange: First, Christ

SINNER SAINT

receives our sinfulness. Second, we receive his righteousness. These two parts are sometimes referred to, respectively, as the non-imputation of sin and the imputation of righteousness. Let's take each of them in turn.

First of all, Christ receives our sinfulness (the non-imputation of sin). "He became sin who knew no sin." At the Cross, Jesus took the sins of the whole world upon his shoulders so that whoever believes in him will not perish but have eternal life (John 3:16). Jesus takes our sin away. Another word for this is forgiveness. One key term in the New Testament used to speak of this (*aphiemi*) means "to dismiss or release someone or something from a place or one's presence," "to release from moral obligation or consequence, *cancel, remit, or pardon.*"[3] When God forgives us, he dismisses our sin from his presence and chooses to remember it no more, casting it as far as the east is from the west (Ps. 103:1). Through forgiveness, our moral accounts are balanced, our sins blotted out, and we are given a clean slate before God. Jesus takes our sins upon himself, bears the penalty for them, endures God's wrath, and receives the punishment we deserved (death). This is forgiveness, and many view it as the entirety of salvation. But in reality, forgiveness is only one side of the coin.

The second side is described in the last half of v. 21: "... so that in him we might become the righteousness of God." In the first part (the non-imputation of sin), Jesus receives our sin. In this second part (the imputation of righteousness), we receive his righteousness. In the first part, our record of debt was canceled, while in

---

[3] *A Greek-English Lexicon of the New Testament and Other Early Christian Literature*, 3rd ed., edited by Walter Bauer, William Frederick Danker, W. F. Arndt, and F. W. Gingrich (Chicago: University of Chicago Press, 2000), s.v. ἀφίημι.

• 62 •

the second part our accounts were filled brimful with credit. What God describes here is much more extravagant than forgiveness, as extravagant as that is. Not only does he take away our sin, but he gives us the immeasurable riches of Christ's righteousness! No longer is our situation such that every personal sin puts our moral ledger in the red. Instead, the blood of Christ guarantees that when God reads my moral ledger it will always be in the black. He hasn't just taken my bad deeds away but has filled my account with Jesus' good deeds, and—through faith—I am treated as if I, myself, were the one who did them! In this great exchange, Jesus receives my mess, and I receive his perfect record. God doesn't just take away my sins, but he gives me something better. He not only negates but credits. Theologian Michael Horton explains how this situation once played out in his own life:

> After my junior year in college, I went to Europe with some friends. Having misjudged my expenses by several digits, I phoned home for help. My parents transferred money from their account to cover outstanding bills and included an additional sum from which I could draw until the end of the trip. Now, was this money, which I was going to draw daily as I needed, strictly speaking, my money? No, it belonged to my parents; nevertheless, because they had transferred it to my account, it was my money. My account was now filled with money I had not earned but which was mine to use nonetheless.[4]

---

[4] Michael Horton, *Putting the Amazing Back into Grace* (Grand Rapids: Baker Books, 2010), 148-155.

SINNER SAINT

When Dad Gives You His Ring

Perhaps the most well-known parable that Jesus tells is that of the Prodigal Son (Luke 15:11-32). You may know it by heart, but the short of it is this. A man had two sons. The younger took his share of the inheritance, squandered it on reckless living (think the 1st century equivalent of The Strip in Las Vegas), and ended up crawling back to his dad in the hopes that he would take him back not as a son, but as a servant. Returning home with a long face, empty-handed, having decimated the family's reputation, the son rehearses his "I'm sorry" speech as he approaches the driveway and makes the final turn toward home. He's fully expecting to be punished, like he deserves. But as he turns into the driveway, something else greets him:

> But while he was still a long way off, his father saw him and felt compassion, and ran and embraced him and kissed him. And the son said to him, "Father, I have sinned against heaven and before you. I am no longer worthy to be called your son." But the father said to his servants, "Bring quickly the best robe, and put it on him, and put a ring on his hand, and shoes on his feet. And bring the fattened calf and kill it, and let us eat and celebrate. For this my son was dead, and is alive again; he was lost, and is found." And they began to celebrate (Luke 15:20b-24).

Instead of being sent to his room, the wayward child is given a party! The older brother (and we) are outraged and scandalized. It is a picture of grace, and of the merciful Father who never withholds his

• 64 •

gifts from his wayward children. He gives grace not to those who deserve it but to those who need it, and no one needs it more than a son presumed dead.

But in the midst of the hubbub of this glorious homecoming, one detail often gets lost: The ring. What's with the ring that the father places on his son's finger? Prior to security ink and Apple ID, when business was transacted in ancient Palestine, a family signet ring legitimized the purchase and sale of goods. By placing the signet ring upon his son's finger, something astounding was happening: the father was restoring his wayward child to the position of sonship with all of the benefits pertaining to that identity. He was giving him access to the family checkbook as proof of his reinstatement into the family. Not only was he forgiven, but he was credited with the righteousness of his father, who bore the consequences of the prodigal's sin. It's a beautiful picture of imputation.

Super-Christians?

Imputation is weird. Full stop. It doesn't make sense, and there are few parallels in everyday life. Also, it grates against every human impulse which demands to be judged on the basis of our merits or demerits rather than those of another on our behalf. To every human sensibility, imputation feels anti-gravitational. Our default operating system treats grace like a virus because it won't allow us to have any skin in the game, so we tend to see righteousness as a power infused rather than a gift imputed. We treat grace like a sort of divine caffeine-boost; a spiritual five-hour-energy that enables us to live holier lives, giving us the extra push that we need to cross the threshold from sinnerhood into sainthood. By default, we view righteousness as the spiritual equivalent of Captain America's super-soldier serum. We get an extra shot of God's grace which transforms us into super-Christians who can single-handedly conquer sin. When the substance is injected, a fundamental change in our nature occurs, activating our willpower and enabling us to cooperate with God.

But Scripture paints a different picture. God's righteousness is not so much a power, but a verdict rendered about us apart from anything we do at all! In fact, the judge who renders the verdict won't even allow our deeds to be admitted into the courtroom, neither the good ones nor the bad ones. In the end, the only evidence admitted into God's courtroom is the shed blood of His Son. Salvation is not dependent on our imperfect, unfinished works, but upon the perfect, finished work of Jesus Christ on our behalf, given to us through faith. As a Christian, then, your relationship with Jesus is the overriding factor that determines who you are.

My Head is Spinning

If this is your first encounter with imputation, let me first say: Congratulations! You survived. Chances are also good that, at this point, you may be feeling disoriented. Perhaps more questions have been raised than answers given. If so, fear not! You are not alone, and we'll tackle those questions shortly. The next chapter aims to clear the weeds by focusing on a handful of myths surrounding the doctrine of the sinner-saint as it pertains to sanctification (i.e. Christian growth). Chapter 7 goes one step further, addressing some of the most common objections to the sinner-saint paradigm. From there, we'll transition from a defensive into an offensive posture, moving toward an inverted understanding of sanctification as downward growth.

CHAPTER 6

Common Myths

SANCTIFICATION IS A MESSY business. Whatever your theological leaning, this is one of the few statements that everyone seems to agree on. It's nonlinear. It's neither consistent nor predictable. As opposed to doctrines like atonement or eschatology or the Trinity which center on God and his work, sanctification has to do with human behavior, which continues to baffle theologians, psychologists, anthropologists, biologists, fathers, wives, employees, bosses, students, teachers, reality show producers, and everyone in between. If the true-crime podcast genre has taught us anything, it's that the basest human desires can lurk behind the most pious facades. Likewise, the most heroic deeds are often accomplished by people who don't fit the classic good citizen mold. Individuals with a history of violence and manipulation will dive into an icy river to save a child from drowning in a sudden burst of selflessness. A nun who has spent her life in a convent is revealed to have perpetrated malicious crimes. And it's not always obvious why. Humans (a heading which Christians, too, fall under) are hard to understand. As the prophet Jeremiah said so long ago, "The heart is deceitful above all things, and desperately sick; who can understand it?" (Jer. 17:9) I prefer Eugene Peterson's rendering in The Message:

> The heart is hopelessly dark and deceitful, a puzzle that no one can figure out. But I, God, search the heart and examine the mind. I get to the heart of the human. I get to the root of things. I treat them as they really are, not as they pretend to be.[1]

With such a diagnosis of our spiritual condition in mind, it's understandable that myths regarding sanctification have crept into Christian circles. And while there is much we don't know, there are some things that Scripture makes clear. So, let's defuse a few of the most commonly-held myths regarding this doctrine. In clearing the minefield, we can set the stage for a more accurate definition to emerge.

Myth #1: The Only Barrier to Sanctification is Bad Deeds

To be clear, bad deeds are, well, bad! Christians should avoid doing them. Be good, not bad. Scripture makes this abundantly clear. So does natural law. If sanctification is, as my own tradition defines it, "the gracious work of the Holy Spirit by which He daily renews me more and more in the image of God through the Word and the

---

[1] Eugene Peterson, *The Message: The Bible in Contemporary Language* (Colorado Springs: NavPress, 2002).

Sacraments,"[2] then the result will be growth in my love for God and hatred toward sin. In Colossians 3, Paul is speaking of our new life in Christ, and he says this:

> If then you have been raised with Christ, seek the things that are above, where Christ is, seated at the right hand of God. Set your minds on things that are above, not on things that are on earth. For you have died, and your life is hidden with Christ in God. When Christ who is your life appears, then you also will appear with him in glory. Put to death therefore what is earthly in you: sexual immorality, impurity, passion, evil desire, and covetousness, which is idolatry. On account of these the wrath of God is coming. In these you too once walked, when you were living in them. But now you must put them all away: anger, wrath, malice, slander, and obscene talk from your mouth. Do not lie to one another, seeing that you have put off the old self with its practices and have put on the new self, which is being renewed in knowledge after the image of its creator (Col. 3:1-10).

Being renewed in the image of Christ, believers are taught to daily fight against the carnal passions that rage within us. We are no longer slaves to sin but slaves to righteousness, and the Holy Spirit empowers us to wage this war. That much is clear.

But bad deeds are not the only barrier to sanctification. There is another hazard, equally pernicious, that flies under the radar. The surprising truth is this: It is not only our bad deeds but our good

---

[2] *An Explanation of Luther's Small Catechism*, 2nd edition, edited by Warren Olsen and David Rinden (Fergus Falls: Faith and Fellowship Press), 84.

deeds that lead to sanctification stagnation. It is those whose confidence is built on their good works that are most susceptible to spiritual pride. In short, those who know that they are bad are better off than those who think they are good. Jesus tells the following parable to illustrate:

> He also told this parable to some who trusted in themselves that they were righteous, and treated others with contempt: "Two men went up into the temple to pray, one a Pharisee and the other a tax collector. The Pharisee, standing by himself, prayed thus: 'God, I thank you that I am not like other men, extortioners, unjust, adulterers, or even like this tax collector. I fast twice a week; I give tithes of all that I get.' But the tax collector, standing far off, would not even lift up his eyes to heaven, but beat his breast, saying, 'God, be merciful to me, a sinner!' I tell you, this man went down to his house justified, rather than the other. For everyone who exalts himself will be humbled, but the one who humbles himself will be exalted" (Luke 18:9-14).

The danger with good deeds is not their intrinsic goodness. The danger, as always, is with the human heart, which takes good things and uses them for evil purposes. The human heart naturally drifts toward self-reliance rather than God-reliance. Spiritually speaking, we'd rather stand on our own two legs. Such a prideful attitude is sin, and while all sin leads to death, the sin of trusting good works has the added danger of appearing holy. Thus, it is easier to get away with. People scoff at the drunkard but applaud the priest, even though the drunkard may be penitent while the priest is puffed up

COMMON MYTHS

in righteousness. Yet Jesus says, "Those who are well have no need of a physician, but those who are sick. I have not come to call the righteous but sinners to repentance" (Luke 5:31-32). Handled by sin-stained human hands, clean things take on a dirty tinge. Our old Adam never leaves without a trace.

Here's an illustration of how this works. In a 2006 study conducted by the National Science Foundation, it was discovered that certain air purifiers actually produce pollution:

> "These [ozonolysis] machines are insidious," said Barbara Riordan, acting chairperson of the California Air Resources Board (ARB), in a warning last year. "Marketed as a strong defense against indoor air pollution, they emit ozone, the same chemical that the ARB [California Air Resources Board] and... U.S. Environmental Protection Agency have been trying to eliminate from our air for decades. More chilling is that some people susceptible to the ill effects of ozone will eagerly bring these Trojan horses home."[3]

In like manner, good deeds filtered through sinner-saints can pollute the clean air of faith with the smog of self-righteousness. Jesus was keenly aware of this danger, which is why he was particularly hard on the Pharisees. He seems to reserve his harshest judgment and most vitriolic language for the legalists because he saw how insidious their spiritual pride was. Their confidence in their good deeds threatened their faith in Christ. To look to our good works for assurance

---

[3] Robert Roy Britt, "Some Air Purifiers Create Smog-Like Conditions," Live Science, 5-9-06, accessed 5-7-24, https://www.livescience.com/755-air-purifiers-create-smog-conditions.html.

naturally means we take our eyes off Jesus. His work and his gifts can take on a superfluous nature while our good deeds take center stage. In contrast, when the law reveals to us just how far off from goodness we are, we despair of our deeds—even the best ones—and instead rest in the finished work of our Savior.

The bottom line is this: Neither avoiding bad deeds nor accruing good deeds automatically gives you a level up in the sanctification game. Furthermore, it is those confident in their goodness—rather than those aware of their badness—who are furthest from the Gospel.

Myth #2: Sanctification is a Two-Way Street

In justification, God does his part. In sanctification, I do my part. That is the unfortunate caricature which has come to dominate the popular Christian imagination. God does the justifying, and we do the sanctifying. Or, to put it a little less synergistically, we—at very least—cooperate with God in sanctification. We work together with him to bring about our transformation and renewal. Functionally speaking, monergism never extends beyond justification.

Scripture, however, tells us that sanctification too is entirely the work of the Holy Spirit. God is doing the verbs while we are the passive recipients. The Apostle Paul puts it this way in 1 Corinthians 6:9-11:

> Or do you not know that the unrighteous will not inherit the kingdom of God? Do not be deceived: neither the sexually immoral, nor idolaters, nor adulterers, nor men who practice homosexuality, nor thieves, nor the greedy, nor drunkards, nor revilers, nor swindlers will inherit the kingdom of God.

> And such were some of you. But you were washed, you were
> sanctified, you were justified in the name of the Lord Jesus
> Christ and by the Spirit of our God.

Notice the passive nature of these verbs in verse 11. They are not things you do. They are things done *to* you. Here the terms justification, sanctification, and "being washed" are all used interchangeably to speak of salvation. The verb for "sanctify" is the same word used in the Lord's prayer for "hallowing" the Lord's name (Matt. 6:9; Luke 11:2). It means "to consecrate or dedicate," "to include a person in the inner circle of what is holy."[4] Ultimately, as Chad Bird says, sanctification is a matter of proximity.[5] To be sanctified means to be brought so near to God through the blood of Christ that the two of you are indistinguishable. In other words, we are brought so close to Jesus through faith that his perfect record, his righteous deeds, and his sinlessness become ours. Jesus bridges the gap between us and God, making a way for us to have peace with the Father. He doesn't bring us forty percent of the way or sixty percent of the way into the Holy of Holies. God doesn't work in fractions. Through faith, we are fully united to Christ (Gal. 2:20-21, Eph. 1:3). You can't get much closer to someone than being united to them. Even in sanctification, God does the heavy lifting.

---

[4] *A Greek-English Lexicon of the New Testament and Other Early Christian Literature,* 3rd ed., edited by Walter Bauer, William Frederick Danker, W. F. Arndt, and F. W. Gingrich (Chicago: University of Chicago Press, 2000), s.v. 'agiazw.

[5] See Old Testament Scholar Chad Bird's talk, "Sanctification: A Matter of Proximity" from the 2022 Here We Still Stand Northwest Arkansas Conference: https://www.youtube.com/watch?v=VOhUH7z5Bzc.

So, then, the question naturally arises: What role do humans play in sanctification? Are we uninvolved? Not at all. There is, of course, a sense in which sanctification is always incomplete on this side of heaven, and to that end that we are encouraged to fight the good fight (2 Tim. 4:7), to work out our salvation with fear and trembling (Phil. 2:12), and to discipline our bodies to keep them under control (1 Cor. 9:27). In the war between the spirit and the flesh we are always active participants. We feel it in our hearts, our guts, our heads, and our wills, often viscerally and with deep emotion. So, we fight. We strive. We try to be better. We work. God is certainly not against working. But any progress we experience in this life can only be attributed to the Holy Spirit. As one author explains: "Progress or growth in the Christian life lies in beginning again, and beginning again means being continually captivated by the unconditionality of the grace of God."[6] We do not sanctify ourselves, though we ourselves are sanctified, and such transformation inevitably involves our affections, wills, and emotions.

Any response on our part, however, is due to the grace of God. The Great Physician always moves first to bring healing to the sin-injured patient, whether through justification or sanctification.

Myth #3: Sanctification is Measurable

Whether it's counting our steps or monitoring our blood pressure or keeping a pulse on the stocks or checking our weight, we love to

---

[6] Gregory A. Boyd and Paul R. Eddy, *Across the Spectrum: Understanding Issues in Evangelical Theology, 2nd edition* (Grand Rapids: Baker Academic, 2009), 165.

measure. We love to quantify. It gives us a feeling of control and feeds the illusion that we are masters of our own fates. If we can put a number to it and see how we compare to others, we can work to increase or decrease it accordingly—whatever "it" is. As helpful as measurements and metrics may be in terms of earthly life, the danger happens when such a framework is copied and pasted into our relationship with God.

In Galatians 5:22 the Apostle Paul says this: "But the fruit of the Spirit is love, joy, peace, patience, kindness, goodness, faithfulness, gentleness, self-control; against such things there is no law." It is interesting to note how he distinguishes the fruit of the spirit from works of the law. Fruit is a very particular kind of thing. It grows on trees and bushes simply by virtue of its species. A blueberry bush bears blueberries; an orange tree bears oranges; an apple tree bears apples. This highlights who does the work in sanctification. The apple tree doesn't try really, really hard to grow apples, and then, when the fruit attains a sufficient level of "apple-ness," it is deemed worthy to be considered an apple tree. The fruit doesn't *make* the apple tree an apple tree. The fruit is simply *evidence* that it is an apple tree. The fruit grows naturally and is the effect, rather than the cause, of the tree's "apple-ness."[7]

The same is true in sanctification. This fruit grows naturally. Counterintuitively, we become more joyful or patient not by trying harder to be joyful and patient, but by rooting ourselves more and more in the source of all good things: Jesus. God promises fruit. What he doesn't promise, however, is that it will always be measurable.

---

[7] This metaphor is derived primarily from Luther's *On the Freedom of the Christian*.

Nowhere does it say that it's our job to quantify growth, to measure it, or to become USDA-approved spiritual fruit inspectors, comparing this year's apples to last year's (am I more patient or kind or loving now than I was a year ago? Depends who you ask!) Nor is it our job to compare our fruit to that of the "apple tree" sitting in the pew next to us (am I at least more patient or kind or loving than them?). While God exhorts us to grow, nowhere does he exhort us to measure.

Myth #4: Sanctification is the Reform of Our Sin Nature

When we talk about "becoming better people" or "improving" as Christians, by that we usually mean living differently. Perhaps we need to develop some new habits, drop some of the old ones, and little by little our old Adam and Eve will be transformed into something beautiful, bright, and new. In other words (or so the old story goes) sanctification is primarily about the reform of our sin nature. Through the law we can whip our old Adam & Eve into shape, trim the spiritual fat, climb the ladder, and rigorously train them to live differently. Sanctification, we are told, is all about how to live differently. The accent is on the Christian life. But growth doesn't always start with life. In fact, a lot of times growth involves death. Not always physical death (although being human certainly means you will die someday), but rather dying to ourselves, our needs, our wishes, our impulses, and our desires. For sinner-saints, the sanctification game is more about dying and rising than it is about reform. To paraphrase what wiser men have said, our old Adam & Eve are strong swimmers and have to be drowned daily. Or, as a former pastor at my parish once put it: our old Adam never gets converted.[8] God doesn't coax our inner sinner into becoming a saint. Instead, he has to put our inner sinner to death to raise us up to new life in Christ. In Romans 6:5-10, the Apostle Paul says this:

> For if we have been united with him in a death like his, we shall certainly be united with him in a resurrection like his. We know that our old self was crucified with him in order that the body of sin might be brought to nothing, so that we would no longer be enslaved to sin. For one who has died has been set free from sin. Now if we have died with Christ, we believe that we will also live with him. We know that Christ, being raised from the dead, will never die again; death no longer has dominion over him. For the death he died he died to sin, once for all, but the life he lives he lives to God. So you also must consider yourselves dead to sin and alive to God in Christ Jesus.

Jesus knew that the Christian life would involve a fair amount of death. When he was instructing his disciples on the cost of following him, he said this: "If anyone would come after me, let him deny himself and take up his cross and follow me. For whoever would save his life will lose it, but whoever loses his life for my sake will find it" (Matt. 16:24-25). Cross-carrying is normative in the life of the disciple. Jesus explained it another way when he was predicting his own death: "Truly, truly, I say to you, unless a grain of wheat falls into the earth and dies, it remains alone; but

---

[8] I'm appreciative of Reverend Willmore Gunderson, late pastor of Elim Lutheran Church, for his use of this phrasing, as quoted to me by a former parishioner.

if it dies, it bears much fruit. Whoever loves his life loses it, and whoever hates his life in this world will keep it for eternal life" (John 12:24-25). What is Jesus driving at? He is saying that we can only experience eternal life in all of its fullness if we are willing to die to our old ways; our old habits and attitudes. The whole "picking up your cross" business might sound sentimental to some, but it's not. Growth involves pruning, and pruning is painful. It hurts, because by definition, it means amputating branches of a tree. In sanctification, Jesus takes his heavenly garden shears to us and starts chopping off parts. He slices right through the sin-sick sections of your heart. He pierces your skin and joints and marrow. He draws blood. He slashes and saws with surgical precision and he won't rest until the tree is healthy. In the short term this is going to hurt. But in the long-term it will bring healing, and a healthy tree that bears good fruit.

In his poem "The Everlasting Mercy," poet John Masefield pictures Jesus like a plowman (named Callow) taking his sharp instrument to the furrows of our diseased hearts, driving the coulter (the part of a metal plough that breaks ground and softens the soil being prepared for planting) deep so that he can grow "the young green corn."

> Old Callow, stooped above the hales,
> Ploughing the stubble into wales.
> His grave eyes looking straight ahead,
> Shearing a long straight furrow red;
> His plough-foot high to give it earth
> To bring new food for men to birth.
> O wet red swathe of earth laid bare,
> O truth, O strength, O gleaming share,

COMMON MYTHS

O patient eyes that watch the goal,
O ploughman of the sinner's soul.
O Jesus, drive the coulter deep
To plough my living man from sleep.[9]

Sanctification is actually death, not life, to our old nature. God is not interested in doing some minor renovations in our hearts. He needs our old Adam and Eve to die so that we can truly live. C.S. Lewis touches on this concept tangentially in *Mere Christianity*, picturing the process of sanctification as a building being torn down and rebuilt:

Imagine yourself as a living house. God comes in to rebuild that house. At first, perhaps, you can understand what He is doing. He is getting the drains right and stopping the leaks in the roof and so on; you knew that those jobs needed doing and so you are not surprised. But presently He starts knocking the house about in a way that hurts abominably and does not seem to make any sense. What on earth is He up to? The explanation is that He is building quite a different house from the one you thought of - throwing out a new wing here, putting on an extra floor there, running up towers, making courtyards. You thought you were being made into a decent little cottage: but He is building a palace. He intends to come and live in it Himself.[10]

---

[9] John Masefield, "The Everlasting Mercy," Project Gutenberg, November 13, 2012, https://www.gutenberg.org/cache/epub/41467/pg41467-images.html.

[10] C.S. Lewis. *Mere Christianity*. (New York: Touchstone, 1996), 175–176.

SINNER SAINT

Whenever God kills us, He does so for our benefit; to make us live. Hosea 6:1-2 says this: "Come, let us return to the Lord; for he has torn us, that he may heal us; he has struck us down, and he will bind us up. After two days he will revive us; on the third day he will raise us up, that we may live before him."

Toward a Positive Definition

In this chapter we've spent a lot of time breaking down what sanctification is not. It is not just about avoiding bad deeds but also about avoiding the self-righteousness that results from good deeds. It is not a two-way street where God does his part, I do my part, and the two of us work together to renovate my soul. It is not measurable in the sense that it cannot be quantified in by human metrics. And it is not about civilizing or domesticating our old Adam & Eve; it is about killing them so that our new nature can emerge. So we know what sanctification is *not*. But while deconstruction is one thing, re-construction is another. A positive definition is now in order. In light of these many common misunderstandings, what is sanctification in sinner-saint terms?

Chapter 10 will explore this question more fully, but for now—at the risk of oversimplifying—sanctification is the messy, nonlinear process by which the Holy Spirit kills and makes alive, transforming us into whom he has already declared us to be in Christ. Sometimes he does this with our cooperation. Sometimes he does it without it. Sanctification is not predicated on human willpower but on God's promise to—like Callow—"plough my living man from sleep" so that he can bring "the young green corn." The tough, old sod of our hearts

• 82 •

resists such work. We grow comfortable and complacent. The roots of our sin grow deep. And nothing short of the coulter of Christ can break up such fallow ground and awaken us to the miracle of grace.

The myths surrounding sanctification are many, and it is far beyond the scope of this book to address them all. Yet by pointing out some of the most common red flags, we move one step closer to embracing the identity of the *simul*. In the next chapter, we'll tackle a few of the most common objections. Does affirming a sinner-saint paradigm produce lazy, "couch-potato Christians?" Is being one hundred percent sinner and one hundred percent saint contrary to fact? Is such a framework too fatalistic, or even a disincentive toward good works? All of this and more is on the docket for Chapter 7.

CHAPTER 7

Responding to Objections

GOD HAS SEEN FIT to bless me with two daughters, ages two and five. My girls love to read, and one of the classics we return to again and again is *Frog & Toad*. In one particular adventure, while baking cookies, the two friends discover the limits of willpower. Frog, alarmed at his lack of self-control, first raises the issue by suggesting they stop eating the delicious cookies they've just baked before they get sick. Agreeing, Toad proposes they eat one last cookie—just to be safe. Several "last cookies" later, Toad cries, "We must stop eating!" As Frog reaches for another, he says, "Yes, we need more willpower," which he goes on to explain to Toad is "trying hard not to do something you really want to do." Summoning all of their remaining willpower, they hide the cookies in a box. They seal the box with a ribbon. They set it high on a shelf. Yet they can't resist temptation. Eventually, in a frustrated fit of passion, Frog tosses the cookies outside where the birds quickly eat them. Toad is saddened that they have no more cookies to eat, but Frog reminds him that now they "have lots and lots of willpower." Done with this willpower nonsense, Toad tells Frog he is going home to bake a cake.[1] It turns out that the reality of the *simul* may apply to amphibians as well.

In a light-hearted way, this story illustrates the struggle we face as sinner-saints. On the one hand, we are beloved, redeemed children of God who sincerely want to do the right thing. As the Holy Spirit daily renews us in God's image, we seek to obey him and strive against sin's mastery. In *Frog &Toad* language, we truly do not want to not eat the cookies. On the other hand, sin lies close at hand and we are susceptible to temptation. Just because I am a Christian doesn't mean the forbidden fruit no longer looks shiny and tastes good. So I find myself indulging in the cookies (or at very least fantasizing about it), even though on another level, I know they are bad for me. Being a sinner-saint doesn't mean that I cease to be a sinner. Rather, it means that—as a repentant and believing sinner—the sins I commit no longer define me. The word of the law no longer has the power to condemn because God speaks a truer and more lasting word over me; the word of the gospel. While the law is penultimate, the gospel is ultimate. I am redeemed, beloved, and forgiven. In Christ, my sins are washed away and I am filled to the brim with his righteousness. Because of the finished work of Jesus on my behalf, God declares me a saint, and when God's performative word declares something to be true, it is true. It's not just a theory. It's not just an opinion. It's not a convenient fiction. His Word is a reality-creating Word, and the new reality is that "I have been crucified with Christ. It is no longer I who

---

[1] Arnold Lobel, *Frog & Toad Storybook Treasury* (New York: HarperCollins, 2014), 96-107.

RESPONDING TO OBJECTIONS

live, but Christ who lives in me. And the life I now live in the flesh I live by faith in the Son of God, who loved me and gave himself for me" (Gal. 2:20). Despite all evidence to the contrary, the wonderful news about the *simul* is that my inner sinner is no longer my primary identity. God makes me a saint. He sees me as a saint. And he treats me as a saint. This new identity is based not on my works but upon Jesus' life, death, and resurrection, received by faith. The condemning voice of the law no longer has authority to pound the gavel and render the verdict, because the gospel tells me something else. It directs my spiritual gaze away from myself and upwards toward the God who saves: "When Satan tempts me to despair and tells me of the guilt within, upward I look and see him there, who put an end to all my sin."[2]

But now the questions start: Isn't this too easy? Isn't it too passive? Isn't it even dangerous? If we affirm the reality of the *simul* with all of its implications, aren't we opening up the door to licentiousness? After all, why would anyone knowingly enter a fight against a foe (in this case sin) that they can never fully defeat? And if our identity as saints rests securely in Christ's finished work and not our own, shall we now live however we want? The fear is that, if we unleash grace in all of its unbridled virility, chaos will ensue. The Apostle Paul faced precisely this accusation on a number of occasions. His response was clear and emphatic: "What shall we say then? Are we to continue in sin that grace may abound? By no means! How can we who died to sin still live in it?" (Rom. 6:1). He repeats himself a few verses later: "What then? Are we to sin because we are not under the law but under grace? By no means!" (Rom. 6:15). In response to

---

[2] Charitie Lees Bancroft, "Before the Throne of God Above," 1863.

the accusation that more grace results in more sin, Paul didn't run back to the law but doubled down on the gospel: "By no means!" He refused to dilute grace by dragging the law back into the salvation equation.

Yet many of our nagging questions remain. So, let's address a few of them.

Couch-Potato Christians?

Perhaps the primary objection to the *simul* is that such a belief will inevitably create lazy Christians who are satisfied with lives of spiritual mediocrity, never seeking to rise above their baser instincts. If our behavior doesn't factor into our identity, we'll simply rest on our laurels, content with our vices and sinful proclivities. Like watching and re-watching a marathon of your favorite TV show late into the night, too much grace lulls us to sleep and instills a sense of complacency when it comes to the sanctification game. It is too fatalistic. The more we say, "Well, we're all just a bunch of helpless, miserable sinners," the less motivation we'll have to fight against sin, and our spiritual muscles will atrophy. It's just too pessimistic, like a terrible coach giving the worst pre-game speech of all time: "All right, bring it in. Losers on three. 1-2-3, LOSERS!" After all, if you are running a spiritual marathon, you don't want a coach who follows you around the track yelling in your ear with a megaphone, "You know, you'll never win! The standard is just too high! You can't do it! You'll never be perfect!" Instead, you want a coach who tells you, you CAN do it. You want a coach who tells you to keep pushing, keep trying, get better, onward and upward! Isn't that what we need in the spiritual realm, too?

RESPONDING TO OBJECTIONS

In response to this reasonable objection, a couple of things can be said.

First, such logic relies more on Aristotelian presuppositions (knowingly or unknowingly) than a biblical worldview, which have infiltrated our thinking to such a degree that we can hardly conceive of an alternative way of thinking. The Greek philosopher Aristotle spoke much about cultivating habits of virtue. For Aristotle, we develop good moral habits in the same way we develop any habit; by repeatedly doing it. The more we practice something, the better we get at it. An aspiring basketball player shoots one hundred shots per day, practicing her form and technique until it becomes second nature. A pianist learns a song through repetition and practice until the notes are embedded in his psyche. Practice makes perfect. According to Aristotle, ethics works the same way. If we cultivate habit through sufficient repetition, we'll eventually become what we do. He puts it this way in his *Nichomachean Ethics:*

> Excellence is an art won by training and habituation: we do not act rightly because we have virtue or excellence, but we rather have these because we have acted rightly; these virtues are formed in man by his doing the actions; we are what we repeatedly do.[3]

So if you want to be more generous, practice doing generous acts until you actually become generous. Want to be a more patient person? Keep pushing yourself to be more patient, and

---

[3] Aristotle, *The Nicomachean Ethics*, ii., 4, quoted in Will Durant, *The Story of Philosophy* (New York: Simon and Schuster, 1926), 87.

eventually, you'll become what you do. For many of us, this seems to go without saying. It's practically axiomatic. How could it be otherwise? But Scripture paints a different picture. Aristotle's underlying assumption (which, I would argue, is also every human's assumption) is that more law produces better behavior. Yet, as we discovered in Chapter 4, God's law actually works in a more counterintuitive way. Its purpose is not what we assume. Remember, "through the law comes knowledge of sin" (Rom. 3:20), and "the law came to increase the trespass" (Rom. 5:20a). Aristotle treats the law as the solution. Paul says it's not. Not only that, but the law kills (2 Cor. 3:6). Remember, the "spiritual CT scan" that the law gives us is the diagnosis, not the cure. While the law may be able to modify behavior (if you tell me to clean my room enough times, I am eventually going to clean my room), it doesn't have the power to sanctify our hearts. Externally it may appear that the law got the job done. After all, the room is now clean. Yet internally, the resentment and bitterness resulting from the law's condemning power only further callouses our hearts. The law doesn't have the power to create love of God and neighbor. Only the gospel can do that, and the gospel is not something to be leveraged but proclaimed. The purpose of the law is to drive us to the gospel. It is never an end in itself, since the gospel—not the law—is "the power of God for salvation to everyone who believes" (Rom. 1:16). For that reason, we can say with Paul, that we are not ashamed of the gospel! The good news of who Jesus is and what he has done out of his great love for us is capable of regenerating our hearts, making us more loving, humble, and selfless people who resemble Jesus more and more.

In a very real sense, all bad behavior stems from not believing the gospel. The more we understand and accept the depths of God's unconditional love for us, the less we'll feel the need to chase after other things. The more we believe in the sufficiency of Christ's atoning work, the less we'll seek to secure our own identities by our own efforts. Good works, then, are no longer motivated by anxiety about whether we are doing enough but by the freedom that results from accepting our identity as God's beloved children. The Gospel puts our hearts at rest, liberating us from the need to pursue God and instead to become his pursued, the ones he hunts down with the intention of blessing (Ps. 23:6a).

The *simul* is not license to sin, but a confession of sin. It's an upfront admission of guilt, without qualification or self-justification. Affirming a sinner-saint paradigm means we don't have to airbrush our lives or morally posture or preen. It means we don't have to minimize the darker side of human nature. We get to bring everything into the light; our thoughts, motivations, the inward attitudes of our hearts, the dark cracks and crevices that we don't want to admit are there—even to ourselves. And we get to know that God forgives it all. In the language of John, we get to step into the light:

> This is the message we have heard from him and proclaim to you, that God is light, and in him is no darkness at all. If we say we have fellowship with him while we walk in darkness, we lie and do not practice the truth. But if we walk in the light, as he is in the light, we have fellowship with one another, and the blood of Jesus his Son cleanses us from all sin (1 John 1:5-7).

There is great freedom in admitting we're frail and broken humans who can't put ourselves back together again. We don't need to keep pretending we're stronger than we really are. The *simul* gives us the language to affirm this, putting to death the myth of the "couch potato Christian."

Shouldn't it be "Saint OR Sinner," Not "Saint AND Sinner?"

Some of us are actually quite comfortable with the terms "sinner" and "saint." They are, after all, lifted straight from Scripture. It's the conjunction between the two terms that we take issue with: that pesky little "and." Generally speaking, humans prefer either/or to both/and statements. Both/and's make us uncomfortable because they require living with tension, and we are not very good at tension. Either/or is less complicated, and allows us to make neat, clean divisions. Some people are good. Some people are bad. Plain and simple. Our task then becomes distinguishing the sinners from the saints. Saint OR sinner would be a much more manageable paradigm, aligning with our propensity to pigeonhole others while defending the moral high ground. The idea of a saint and sinner coexisting in the same individual is just too messy to maintain.

The problem with being one or the other, though (either "sinner" or "saint") is twofold. First, if we're only sinners, then we're lost and damned, "for the wages of sin is death" (Rom 6:23a). Sin separates us from God, we are declared "guilty," and sentenced to an eternity in Hell. Second, if we're only saints, then we have no ongoing need for Christ and the forgiveness he won at the Cross. Sainthood has been attained,

RESPONDING TO OBJECTIONS

salvation secured, and Jesus' work is done here. He can pack his bags and go home. That's where a "saint OR sinner" paradigm ultimately leads. The *AND* is absolutely essential if we are to look clear-eyed at the sin-stained reflection staring back at us in the mirror. But the greater truth is that Christ stands between us and the mirror, and his perfect, spotless, holy reflection becomes ours through faith. The challenge of the Christian life is to learn to see ourselves as our Heavenly Father sees us.

In season 2 of the popular TV show "This is Us," a poignant moment between a father and his daughter illustrates this truth powerfully. Jack is recording his teenage daughter Kate singing in her room as she practices for an audition. When she catches sight of him, she is surprised and angry. She struggles with self-image issues and can't stand to see or hear herself on camera. Jack tries to convince her. "I thought that if you saw how great you were you'd re-consider sending in a video... it would break my heart if you didn't want to be on camera because you don't realize how beautiful you are," he says. But Kate storms off. "Dad, stop! You saying stuff like that was fine when I was a kid. But I'm older now and I just don't see myself the way you see me." But in a later scene she has a change of heart. "I watched the tape," she tells her dad. "Okay," he says. A pause ensues, until his daughter finally pipes up: "Don't ever stop," she says. Jack gives her a confused look, so she explains. "Don't stop trying to make me see myself the way you see me." "Okay, Katie girl," Jack reassures her. "I won't stop."[4] Our Heavenly Father won't

---

[4] *This Is Us*, season 2, episode 13, "That'll Be The Day," directed by Uta Briesewitz, written by Dan Fogelman, Kay Oyegun, and Don Roos, featuring Milo Ventimiglia, Mandy Moore, and Sterling Brown, aired January 22, 2018, NBC.

stop either. He won't stop trying to help us see ourselves the way he sees us.

We are saints and sinners. The moment we cease to be a *simul* (saint AND sinner) is the moment we cease to need Jesus.

I WAS a Sinner, but NOW I'm a Saint—Right?

Another common objection has to do with the present-tense aspect of the *simul*. "Sure, maybe I used to be a sinner (past tense)," we think. "But now (present tense) I'm a saint." After all, Paul's epistles don't open with the salutation "To the *sinners* who are in Ephesus" but rather "To the *saints* who are in Ephesus." The picture painted of the Christian life is upward trending, it is argued. We leave the sinner behind and begin to inhabit the saint. It's like metamorphosis, where the butterfly leaves its caterpillar husk behind in the cocoon and flies away, never to revisit it. Likewise, we start out sinful at conversion, but little by little, our spiritual muscles bulk up until we attain sufficient strength to leave the cocoon of our sinner behind and fly away on the wings of a saint. At the risk of mixing metaphors, eventually we cast aside the training wheels of Jesus as we reach independence and learn to ride unaided.

The problem with this picture is that if it is true, as a rule we would expect elderly Christians to be noticeably better-behaved than younger ones. Yet life experience teaches us this is not universally the case. We have all encountered fellow believers who in their old age became more bitter, calloused, and closed-off than they were earlier in life. On the flip side, others become more soft and compassionate as they age. Conversely, we've all encountered young, brash

• 94 •

RESPONDING TO OBJECTIONS

Christians puffed up with pride, while we also run across two-year-olds with a greater dependence on God than the sturdiest lifelong Sunday School teacher. How are we to understand this? Gerhard Forde makes this humorous yet incisive observation:

> As I get older and death draws nearer, I don't seem to be getting better. I get a little more impatient, a little more anxious about having perhaps missed what this life has to offer, a little slower, harder to move, a little more sedentary and set in my ways. Am I making progress? Well, maybe it seems as though I sin less, but that may only be because I'm getting tired! It's just too hard to keep indulging the lusts of youth. Is that sanctification? I wouldn't think so! One should not, I expect, mistake encroaching senility for sanctification![5]

He's touching on something important. There is no predictable, correlative relationship between old age and sanctification. Sinners and saints come in all shapes and sizes, from the cradle roll to the senior citizens brigade.

The other difficulty with this objection is that, if sin is something to be gotten past in this life, what need do we have of the Cross? Is forgiveness something we still require, or have we jumped that hurdle? If we WERE sinners but are NOW saints, then the Cross becomes a crutch that we eventually outgrow as our spiritual muscles strengthen.

---

[5] Gerhard Forde, "The Lutheran View," *Five Views of Sanctification*, ed. Donald L. Alexander (Downers Grove, IL: InterVarsity, 1989), 31-32.

Isn't the *Simul* Contrary to Fact?

Of all of the objections raised, this might be the most serious. It is argued that the sinner-saint paradigm is a convenient legal fiction where God tells a white lie about us. He knows we sin. He knows we are sinners. Yet he declares us righteous, which is contrary to fact. We are not, in-point-of-fact, righteous. Yet he ascribes righteousness to us despite the fact that all evidence points to the contrary. How can God do this? How can a God of justice, who always judges rightly and is in very nature truth himself, choose to make a decision based on untruth? It's dishonest.

This objection, however, actually rests upon an anemic understanding of God's Word and a failure to distinguish the massive difference between God's speech and our speech. When human beings speak, our words operate in a particular way to do a particular thing. Our words can convey information, as when a teacher instructs her class. Our words can make demands, as when a parent tells his child to do her homework. Our words can do many things. The Word of God, however, is a categorically different kind of word. It is performative. It actually does something. God's Word not only says what it does, but it does what it says. His Word is powerful and efficacious, and we see "The Word of the Lord" operative in this way throughout Scripture. God's first words in the Bible, "Let there be light" (Gen. 1:3), operate in this way. God speaks and it happens. When it comes to human beings, however, something more than mere speech is required to make light happen. As Tim Keller helpfully illustrates, we could say "Let there be light" in a dark room, but we'd then have to go over and flip the light switch. God's speech is different. It has

RESPONDING TO OBJECTIONS

the ability to bring into existence things that didn't exist before, and light is the first example of this. This pattern is prevalent throughout all of the Bible. Pay close attention whenever you see "the Word of the Lord" appear in Scripture, because it means things are about to happen. God's Word doesn't just convey information. It is living and active and powerful, separating joints and marrow (Heb. 4:12), piercing us (Luke 2:35), hammering us (Jer. 23:29), giving life (Ps. 119:25), making dry bones live (Ezek. 37:1-14), and it never returns void but always accomplishes its purpose (Isa. 55:11).

God's Word is more than *in*formative. It is *per*formative. We see this in the prophets when God's Word brings some to repentance and hardens others. We see this in Jesus' parables when some believe and some doubt. We see this when the storm flares up on the sea of Galilee and Jesus calms the waves with just a word. And in Romans we read that God's Word actually has the power to create faith in the hearts of its hearers:

> How then will they call on him in whom they have not believed? And how are they to believe in him of whom they have never heard? And how are they to hear without someone preaching? And how are they to preach unless they are sent? As it is written, "How beautiful are the feet of those who preach the good news!" But they have not all obeyed the gospel. For Isaiah says, "Lord, who has believed what he has heard from us?" So faith comes from hearing, and hearing through the word of Christ (Rom. 10:14-17).

OK. Got it. God's Word does stuff. But how does this apply to the "legal fiction" objection to the *simul*? Simply this: When God declares

• 97 •

us righteous, he is not speaking contrary to fact. Because of the creative power of God's Word, his declaration that we are saints is functionally the same as his making us saints. He doesn't just call us something we are not. Instead, he names us what we are. He brings about a new birth, and—as anyone who has witnessed a birth can attest—there is nothing fictitious about it. His Word fundamentally changes reality, bringing about a situation that didn't exist prior to him speaking, and the former categories are no longer constitutive of our being.

"God is not man, that he should lie, or a son of man, that he should change his mind" (Num. 23:19). In the sinner-saint paradigm there is no room for fiction. Our new identity in Christ is no joke. It is as real as the Old Rugged Cross at Calvary.

From Defense to Offense

Thus far we've approached the *simul* primarily from an apologetic, defensive posture. In the next few chapters, we'll begin making the switch to offense. We'll speak more about what the *simul* is, continuing to build a positive case for sanctification that views Christian growth as primarily a downward-thrusting activity. Before we get there, however, we'll take off our apologist's hat for a moment and don that of a pastor. This whole discussion, after all, is not about an ethereal theological concept but about flesh-and-blood human beings. So how does the sinner-saint paradigm affect our everyday relationships, particularly our relationships with fellow Christians? Might it create space for mutual understanding and compassion in a way that other systems fail to do? Chapter 8 seeks to address those questions.

CHAPTER 8

You're Not Alone

IN THE FIRST CHAPTER, I mentioned my personal frustrations with trying to get my daughters down for bedtime. Well, we've now hit Chapter 8, and I'm still struggling. If my objective in writing a book on sanctification was to become more sanctified, it seems my strategy was a miserable failure. There's just something about that time of day which causes the whole family to spiral. Everyone is low on patience, yet somehow strong on willpower, seeking to impose our wills on one another as we battle it out for the upper hand. From deciding on an appropriate snack, to debating proper tooth-brushing strategies, to picking out pajamas, to determining how many books and which ones to read, every decision is poised for potential conflict. Both parties approach the battlefield with swords drawn, ready to parry and counter to ensure that our respective wishes are met. In an argument between a five-year-old and a thirty-eight-year-old, usually the thirty-eight-year-old wins. Usually. But at what cost to our littlest neighbors?

Recently I had a proud parenting moment. I don't have as many of those as I'd like. I don't recall specifically how it came about, though in all likelihood it was due less to any personal holiness on my part and more to the fact that I was just too tired to fight anymore. In the midst of a particularly heated exchange with my four-year-old, I had the Holy-Spirit-granted presence of mind to call a temporary cease-fire. I stopped talking, got down on her level, and looked my daughter in the eye. And something changed in her demeanor. I saw it. Some almost-imperceptible shift in her posture, a slight relaxing of the shoulders, and she was there—present, really present—with me. We were meeting on the same plane, and we saw each other for what we were: sinners in need of grace. It wasn't that I was right and she was wrong. We were both guilty parties, Christians simultaneously redeemed and being changed by Jesus yet still wrestling mightily with the selfish passions waging war within. Even my more objectively sensible stance regarding bedtime was no excuse, because it came from a place of fear. I feared losing control of the situation. As a parent, I desired sovereignty. But in that moment when we met on neutral ground, I caught a glimpse of life through the eyes of a four-year-old. What would it be like to have your eyesight fixed at 2' 6", and to always feel so limited in your understanding? What would it be like to continually have your ideas ignored or at very least glossed over? What would it be like to feel unseen and unimportant? What would it be like to walk a mile in her shoes (or, more precisely, in her sparkly pink plastic princess slippers)? In short, what would it be like to extend compassion to a fellow sufferer caught in the trap of sin?

It is one thing to grasp the concept of the *simul* theologically. It is quite another to experience it personally. One of the beautiful byproducts of the *simul* is that it creates space for compassion. All are sinners. All fall short. That means everyone (including Christians) are in the same boat. We are all infected with some variant of the disease called sin. Everyone experiences symptoms and wrestles through their competing impulses on a daily basis, sometimes winning and sometimes losing. But whatever the final tally in your win and loss columns may be, we've all felt the internal tug-of-war. We've all done battle with ourselves. And that creates a common understanding; a shared vocabulary wherein spiritual warriors can safely share their stories. It turns out we are not so different after all, and compassion is the binding agent that holds us together. The *simul* has much to tell us, not just about who we are, but about who Christ is.

Compassion

Compassion seems to be in short supply these days. At best, it is treated as a necessary evil. It is seen as a kind of last-ditch, Hail Mary effort that might need to be temporarily deployed to carry someone through a rough patch. But it's certainly not meant to be our default posture. If a friend is weak and hurting, for example, you may treat them with compassion until they become strong again, but that is only for a season. At worst, compassion is treated as a vice for the weak-willed and weak-minded. Strong, independent, mature people don't need the safety net of compassion. Some have gone so far as to label compassion a sin.

But Jesus thought differently.

In one of his more well-known parables in Luke 10:25-37, Jesus tells his famous story of the Good Samaritan. In response to a lawyer seeking to justify himself, Jesus answered his question of "who is my neighbor?" in this way: A man on his way to Jericho from Jerusalem was beaten and left by the side of the road for dead. Along came a priest

SINNER SAINT

and a Levite (aka the "good guys"), both of whom completely ignored him and passed over to the other side. Then a Samaritan enters stage left. This is where the parable gets interesting because Samaritans and Jews did not get along. We would expect this Samaritan to behave similarly to the priest and Levite toward the injured Jew, if not worse. But that's not how the story goes. Instead, the text reads that "when he saw him, he had compassion" (Luke 10:33). The verb for "had compassion" or "had pity" (*splagchnizomai*) means that he was moved in his most inward parts. In Greek, the word refers to the bowels or kidneys. In other words, when the Samaritan saw this suffering Jew he felt it in his guts. In modern-day language we might say his heart went out to him. But this compassion wasn't just a feeling; it also translated into action. He picked him up in all of his bloody mess, tenderly treated and bandaged his wounds, placed him on his horse, and had him nursed back to health at the local inn, paying the man's medical bill out of his own pocket. Jesus concludes the parable by putting a question to the lawyer (Luke 10:36-37): "'Which of these three, do you think, proved to be a neighbor to the man who fell among the robbers?' He said, 'The one who showed him mercy.' And Jesus said to him, 'You go, and do likewise.'"

Considering the context of the lawyer's original question, the point of the parable is clear: Jesus is our good Samaritan. He finds us on the side of the road, bruised and bloodied by our own sin, unable to heal ourselves. And he has compassion. He shows us mercy. Romans 5:6-8: "For while we were still weak, at the right time Christ died for the ungodly. For one will scarcely die for a righteous person—though perhaps for a good person one would dare even to die—but God shows his love for us in that while we

• 102 •

YOU'RE NOT ALONE

were still sinners, Christ died for us." For Jesus, compassion isn't a last-ditch effort or a necessary evil but the very face of grace. If Jesus had a website, compassion would be on the homepage. He front-loads compassion rather than tacking it on at the end of his interactions with people as a kind of asterisk. To broken sinners deserving nothing but wrath and condemnation, eternally etched onto the face of Jesus is an expression of compassion. He feels for us. He identifies deeply with our suffering, even the suffering we bring on ourselves by our own sin. He *splagchnizomai's* us. And he calls us to go and do likewise.

Compassion isn't a once-and-done thing with Jesus, either. It's all over the New Testament. When he encountered the crowds of people during his teaching ministry in Galilee, "he had compassion for them, because they were harassed and helpless, like sheep without a shepherd" (Matt. 9:36). A few chapters later, grieving the death of his cousin, Jesus withdraws to a desolate place to be alone, taking a boat out on the Sea of Galilee. But "when He went ashore he saw a great crowd, and he had compassion on them and healed their sick" (Matt. 14:14). Soon after, in the feeding of the four thousand, "Jesus called his disciples to him and said, 'I have compassion on the crowd because they have been with me now three days and have nothing to eat. And I am unwilling to send them away hungry, lest they faint on the way'" (Matt. 15:32). In the village of Nain, Jesus encountered a widow whose son had just died, "and when the Lord saw her, he had compassion on her and said to her, 'Do not weep'" (Luke 7:13). Finally, in the parable of the prodigal son, the merciful father (representing our Heavenly Father) looks out from the balcony and sees his long-lost prodigal at the end of the driveway. His reaction is immediate: "... But while he was still a long way off, his father saw him and felt compassion, and ran and embraced him and kissed him" (Luke 15:20). In his heart of hearts, Jesus' deepest impulse toward sinners is compassion. Is ours?

Common Responses to Christian Mediocrity

The way we respond to Christian mediocrity or non-transformation—whether we encounter it in our neighbor or the person staring back at us in the mirror—tells us a lot about what we actually believe. These responses typically fall somewhere along a spectrum: We judge, ignore, or justify.

A common knee-jerk reaction when we see a fellow believer persisting in sin is judgment. It has been said, fairly or unfairly, that Christians tend to shoot their wounded. The fact that such a stereotype even exists is a sad commentary on the state of our witness to a watching world. We have failed to heed Jesus' reminder that "by this all people will know that you are my disciples, if you have love for one another" (John 13:35). In our efforts to "run with endurance the race that is set before us" (Heb. 12:1), there is a tendency to "leave the lost and dead behind."[1] The journey of sanctification is not for the faint of heart, and the farther we travel along the road, the more we separate the wheat from the chaff. When a brother or sister in Christ falls, too often there is haughtiness in our eyes rather than tears. We treat the arena of faith like a kind of gladiator's coliseum; not everyone will

---

[1] Breaking Benjamin, "I Will Not Bow," track 2 on *Dear Agony*, House of Loud Studios, 2009, compact disc.

survive the fight. Francis Schaeffer speaks of this in the context of Christians disagreeing with one another, but his principle applies to the subject of compassion as well: "The world must observe that, when we must differ with each other as true Christians, we do it not because we love the smell of blood, the smell of the arena, the smell of the bullfight, but because we must for God's sake. If there are tears when we speak, then something beautiful can be observed."[2]

Too often we jump to the conclusion that the existence of ongoing sin in the life of a believer indicates a lack of willpower on their part. But it may not be so simple. Simeon Zahl asks this astute question:

> Who are we to say that what looks and feels like troubling 'non-transformation' does not also entail a deep and sanctified humility in the eyes of God 'unto whom... all desires [are] known and from whom no secrets are hid'? Who are we to say that what looks and feels like saintliness does not hide deep subtleties of pride and ambivalence? Under such circumstances, it is better to develop a theology of sanctification that sees grace as indexed to the very 'worst' Christians than to try to establish who has and has not been transformed by the Spirit and how far.[3]

Let's put skin on this theology and look at some everyday examples. When someone cuts me off on the highway, I automatically assume it's because they are simply a bad or distracted driver. The

---

[2] Francis Schaeffer, *The Mark of a Christian* (Downers Grove, IL: InterVarsity, 1970), 26-27.

[3] Simeon Zahl, *The Holy Spirit and Christian Experience* (Oxford, Oxford University Press, 2020), 230.

thought never crosses my mind that he or she may have received a bad medical diagnosis earlier in the day so his or her mind is overcome with grief and suffering. Or when a telemarketer interrupts my supper, my voice instinctively hardens as I abruptly judge them for their impudence and hang up the phone. Not once do I think that they too have a family and may be struggling to feed them by submitting themselves to a barrage of ill-treatment similar to the one I just administered. We assume a lot, and this is especially true when it comes to our fellow brothers and sisters in Christ. As Jesus knew so well, we focus on the speck in our brother's eye while ignoring the plank in our own (Matt. 7:1-6). There is much we don't see, and God is primarily concerned about the state of our hearts rather than the outward actions themselves. Judgment comes naturally to us. Compassion does not.

At other times, rather than judge sin, we ignore it. The ongoing presence of sin in the life of believers is just too uncomfortable to acknowledge so we pretend it's not there at all. Instead, we focus on living the victorious Christian life. "Let's not fixate on the negative," we think. "That road leads to despair. The Christian life should be more hopeful. After all, Jesus didn't stay on the Cross. He rose from the dead! We're Easter Christians, not Good Friday Christians." Well, yes and no. Yes, Christians live in hope of the Resurrection with the sure knowledge that one day suffering will end and we'll spend eternity with Jesus in the new heavens and the new earth. But no, because on this side of heaven we always live in the shadow of the cross. All of life is a kind of Good Friday as we await the second coming and the final resurrection. This is why Paul adamantly asserts to the Corinthian church that he "decided to know nothing among you except Jesus Christ and him crucified" (1 Cor. 2:2). "Really, Paul?" we think. "Nothing but Jesus crucified? That sounds kind of gloomy. What about Jesus risen? What about Jesus glorified?" But Paul is not denying the resurrection with this statement. He's simply making the point that the sacrificial death of Jesus is at the center of the Christian faith. And not only that, but cross-carrying is actually the defining mark of the disciple (Matt. 16:24). We are not theologians of glory, but theologians of the cross. Ignoring or glossing over sin does nothing but sweep it under the rug. It doesn't deal with the actual problem.

At still other times when we encounter Christian mediocrity, rather than judging or ignoring it we justify it. We defend it, refusing to acknowledge it for the sin that it is. We explain it away. "My actions were justified. I'm just under a lot of stress right now. We all have our limits. How could I have done otherwise? It's completely understandable. I did the best I could. What more could be expected of me? Nobody's perfect!" Statements like these indicate we're in the realm of self-justification, trying to prove to ourselves and others that we're at very least no worse than the person in the pew next to us. The more evidence we can marshal in our defense, the more likely the judge will pound down his gavel and declare us "innocent." At root, it's an avoidance tactic, detracting attention from our failures by shining the spotlight on others and theirs. In our minds, somehow their guilt frees us from our culpability. But the logic just doesn't hold up. A man accused of killing a person in Montana would never defend himself by pointing out that a second murderer in an unrelated case killed two people in Georgia. The "worse" sins of another—whether real or imagined—do not exonerate us of ours. The Christian's ongoing struggle with sin cannot be solved by justifying or excusing it.

• 107 •

The bottom line is that all of these responses only further alienate us from our brothers and sisters in Christ. If Christian mediocrity is viewed as an anomaly, it will always lead us to treat one another as outsiders struggling independently. But if it is viewed as a struggle in which every member of the family of faith participates, we can come to see ourselves as co-combatants fighting against a common enemy. We are on the same side. Any blow another believer suffers is a blow to me, too. There is no time for friendly fire when you're fighting for survival from a foxhole. We are fellow sufferers born into this world wounded by sin and susceptible to the same snares of the world, the flesh, and the devil. And when our brother or sister in Christ is wounded and bleeding, we don't draw attention to the wound. Instead, we have compassion on them, bandage them up, and carry them to our Great Physician so that he can remove the bullet, cleanse their wound, and heal them. Compassion is key to this whole endeavor.

Touching Vocal Cords

A scene from the 2021 film *Coda* captures this spirit of compassion beautifully. The film centers around the Rossis, a fishing family from Gloucester, Massachusetts. Every member of the family (Dad - Frank, Mom - Jackie, and brother - Leo) is deaf except for their daughter Ruby. She is their sole connection to the outside world (the "hearing" world), and they rely on her to translate for them. In fact, their livelihood largely depends on it, even though Ruby is only seventeen. One day, after signing up for the school choir, Ruby discovers she has a talent for singing. Her voice is so extraordinary that her teacher encourages her to audition at Berklee College of Music in Boston. She's never done anything like this before, and she is caught between two worlds. She feels pressure from her family to say no to this opportunity since they need her at home to help with the business. Her family has no real reference point for her experience. They can't hear, so the beauty of music is lost on them. Likewise, she has no frame of reference for their experiences as deaf people living in a "hearing" world. It seems impossible for either party to empathize with the other. In one powerful scene, however, the dam breaks. Ruby and her father Frank are alone in the backyard, sitting on the tailgate of his pickup after one of her concerts. They converse together in sign language, and it's evident that Frank genuinely wants to understand his daughter's passion for music. He just doesn't know how. So Ruby begins to sing. He lip reads for a while, but then he gently moves his hands to her neck so he can actually feel the vibrations of her vocal cords. A sudden change transforms his face, and he is overcome with emotion, his eyes filling with tears. He hugs his girl and kisses her forehead. For the first time, Frank truly understands Ruby's love for music.

This is a glimpse of what divine compassion looks like. When Jesus empathizes with us, he reaches out his nail-scarred hands and gently touches us, feeling the hurt and pain and resonating with what we resonate with. We don't have to explain ourselves. He knows it all before we even say a word. He is there with us, fully present in our situation. As the author of Hebrews says: "For we do not have a high priest who is unable to sympathize with our weaknesses, but one who in every respect has been tempted as we are, yet without sin. Let us then with confidence draw near to the throne of grace, that we may receive mercy and find grace to help in time of need" (Heb. 4:15-16).

Jesus takes compassion on us, or *splagchnizomais'* us in his inward parts. When we understand the *simul* as a category that applies to all Christians, it opens up a world of compassion. It's not that we are saints and our neighbors are sinners, nor vice versa. Every member of God's ragamuffin family is a redeemed sinner being transformed into the image of Christ. We are all pilgrims, and we can find mutual comfort and consolation in the company of other sinner-saints making their way toward the Heavenly City.[4]

In the next chapter, we'll take another look at the internal civil war in the hearts of believers, but this time from a different angle. If it is true that such tension is the norm rather than the exception throughout the Christian life, how can we learn to walk faithfully, neither throwing in the towel nor expecting sinless perfection? We'll take a scalpel to those questions in Chapter 9, dissecting them in detail as we move toward re-defining sanctification as "downward growth" in Chapter 10.

---

[4] Term borrowed from John Bunyan's classic work *Pilgrim's Progress.*

CHAPTER 9

Embracing the Battle

"I DID IT AGAIN."

James had struggled with the same sin for years with little visible progress, and he didn't know where to turn any more. He was a Christian. He knew that much. He'd been baptized and raised in the church. To the question, "Do you believe that Jesus died and rose again to save you from your sins?" he would respond with a resounding YES every time. There had never been a moment in his life when he'd not been a follower of Jesus. He'd never walked away from the faith. He'd never had any big, dramatic bottoming out experience. As far as anyone else knew, he was a strong, faithful churchgoer, married and with four kids. He even taught Sunday School. Yet no matter what technique he applied, no matter how hard he prayed, and no matter who held him accountable, he always seemed to fall back into old habits. Sure, he'd have good streaks when he successfully avoided this particular sin for months on end. At times, it even seemed like he may have turned over a new leaf. But then in a moment of weakness, like a dog to its vomit, he would run back to indulge the toxic behavior once again. "It just seems inevitable," he said in frustration.

"I know God says he'll always provide a way out of temptation, but I just don't know anymore. I can't seem to kick this one. I feel like I've tried everything, but I can't stop the impulse. What do I do? Does this mean I'm not really a Christian? Do I need more willpower? How could God forgive someone like me? I know he says seventy times seven, but that can't apply in this case, right? I've been a Christian my whole life, and I should be better at this point. The fact that I'm not, must point to a weakness in my faith. What am I doing wrong?!"

How would you advise James? What would you say? What passages of Scripture would you point to? How would you pray for him? The way you answer those questions will give you a pretty good idea of where you land in this whole discussion of the *simul*; the idea that Christians live a "split" existence in the sense that we are simultaneously redeemed by Christ (100% saint) yet continue to wrestle mightily with sin (100% sinner). What do we do with this tension?

It Hurts!

Humans have a tendency to interpret tension or pain as a sign that something has gone drastically wrong and should be immediately corrected. To be sure, in certain cases this is true. When your hand comes in contact with a hot burner, pain receptors warn you to remove your hand from the stovetop as quickly as possible. Pain can act as a self-preservation mechanism. Yet there are other varieties of pain. The pain you feel trying to max out on the bench press isn't necessarily an indication that you should stop pushing yourself. Instead, it is a necessary part of the training process, as muscle tissue is broken down so that new tissue can grow back stronger. Or

EMBRACING THE BATTLE

consider undergoing physical therapy after a debilitating accident. As you grip the walker and try to move your legs for the first time in a month, the fact that every cell in your body is screaming for you to stop because it hurts is no reason to actually stop. Your physical therapist will encourage you to push through the pain because it means your body is doing its job. It boils down to this: Is pain (tension) a red flag telling us to stop or a green light telling us to push through?

This analogy relates to our discussion of sanctification in the following way: As Christians undergo sanctification under the knife of the Great Physician, at some point we have to make a decision: Is the painful tension I'm feeling between my old and new natures a warning flag telling me to course correct or is it something else? To put it bluntly: Is the inner struggle of the sinner-saint cause for concern? Our knee-jerk response is to say yes. Our automatic reflex when we feel ourselves painfully torn between two competing desires is to resolve it by veering into one ditch or the other. It's just too uncomfortable. Human beings don't do tension very well. But is it possible that, in our efforts to resolve the tension and avoid the pain, we actually do ourselves a disservice? Could it be that the intensity of the inner struggle we experience isn't so much a spiritual fire alarm as it is a sign of life? One source offers this particularly insightful yet surprising assessment: "As long as the struggle is evident, a person can take assurance that this Spirit [the Holy Spirit] is still present and active. The time to worry is when the struggle ceases, when a person no longer cares whether one is sinning or not."[1] In other words,

---

[1] Robert Kolb & Charles P. Arand, *The Genius of Luther's Theology: A Wittenberg Way of Thinking for the Contemporary Church* (Grand Rapids: Baker Academic, 2008), 127.

the battle between the old and the new—this internal civil war we are continually caught in the middle of—should be embraced rather than shunned. It should be seen as normative for the Christian life.

The God-Wrestler

The story of Jacob's name change is one for the ages. You can imagine him in his later years, gathering his children and grandchildren around, Manasseh and Ephraim hopping up onto his lap and begging, "Please, Grandpa? Tell us the story about how God changed your name one more time!"

It came about like this: Jacob, whose name means "he grasps the heel", lived up to his namesake. Whether it was pocketing his brother's birthright or tricking his father into blessing him, Jacob had a knack for knavery. It was practically his love language. Esau, understandably, didn't take too kindly to this and sought to kill Jacob. So Jacob fled. And twenty years passed with neither brother seeing hide nor hair of the other. Eventually, however, the time for mending fences arrived, and their two paths were set to cross. Jacob, in great fear and distress at this prospect, attempted to placate his brother with a series of gifts, certain that Esau would still be angry after all these years. He sent his messengers and possessions and family ahead, remaining behind to wrestle his own demons. Or, rather, to wrestle with God. What followed was a life-changing encounter:

> And Jacob was left alone. And a man wrestled with him until the breaking of the day. When the man saw that he did not prevail against Jacob, he touched his hip socket, and Jacob's

EMBRACING THE BATTLE

hip was put out of joint as he wrestled with him. Then he said, "Let me go, for the day has broken." But Jacob said, "I will not let you go unless you bless me." And he said to him, "What is your name?" And he said, "Jacob." Then he said, "Your name shall no longer be called Jacob, but Israel, for you have striven with God and with men, and have prevailed." Then Jacob asked him, "Please tell me your name." But he said, "Why is it that you ask my name?" And there he blessed him. So Jacob called the name of the place Peniel, saying, "For I have seen God face to face, and yet my life has been delivered." The sun rose upon him as he passed Penuel, limping because of his hip. Therefore to this day the people of Israel do not eat the sinew of the thigh that is on the hip socket, because he touched the socket of Jacob's hip on the sinew of the thigh (Gen. 32:24-32).

Much could be said about Jacob's mysterious encounter with God. In many ways we're left with more questions than answers. For our purposes, though, it is enough to point out that it was only after wrestling with God that Jacob finally found the courage to face his brother. Jacob the heel-grasper was transformed into Jacob the God-wrestler, because he had striven with God and with men and had prevailed. In the context of battle, the verb for "had prevailed" can also mean "overcome." It is the same word used by Goliath in 1 Samuel 17:9 when he issues his challenge to the Israelites, laying out the terms of battle. Jacob wrestles God and overcomes, ultimately receiving a blessing. But he is left with a limp, wounded for the rest of his life. On the shores of the Jabbok that night, Jacob wrestled against the fiercest adversary of his life—and that adversary was God himself.

• 115 •

What are we to make of this? It is one thing to wrestle with fears and doubts and insecurities. It is something else to wrestle with God; to perceive him as your enemy. Yet try as we might to avoid this uncomfortable reality, the truth remains that this type of experience is anything but anomalous. We've all been there. We've all walked through seasons of trial when it seemed as though God was against us, actively working to frustrate our plans and inflicting lasting damage in the process. Yet notice the end result. Jacob leaves with a limp, but he also leaves with a blessing. Far from being the exception, such gut-wrenching spiritual dislocations are actually part of God's proper work. We know this because of the cross. It is for good reason that the cross is the enduring symbol of the Christian faith: "For I decided to know nothing among you except Jesus Christ and him crucified" (1 Cor. 2:2). At the cross, we see the sins of the world forgiven and salvation won, yet the instrument through which this takes place is a tortured, brutally beaten figure wrenched from his proper place and pinned to a tree like some sick sort of trophy. But John proclaims again and again that it is only through the crucifixion that Jesus will actually be glorified (see John 7:39, 12:16, 12:23, and especially John 13:31-32). The cross is not just a hurdle to be overcome on the way to the resurrection. It is not *in spite of* or *after* the cross that Jesus is glorified. It is, in fact, *through* the cross that his hour of glorification arrives. The cross is the lodestone of the Christian faith.

In the same way that Jacob's hip suffered dislocation at the hands of his Savior, we too are called to undergo spiritual dislocations of sorts as we resist God's painful work in our lives. Yet pain is not the end game. In God's economy, it holds a kind of penultimate purpose because, ultimately, it is for our healing. It is for our benefit. God's goal is to bless us, and often this comes through a good old-fashioned spiritual wrestling match. We can take comfort, however, that even God's wounding is for our healing: "See now that I myself am he! There is no god besides me. I put to death and I bring to life, I have wounded and I will heal, and no one can deliver out of my hand" (Deut. 32:39 NIV). In the midst of his great suffering, this message came through loud and clear to God's servant Job as well: "Behold, blessed is the one whom God reproves; therefore despise not the discipline of the Almighty. For he wounds, but he binds up; he shatters, but his hands heal" (Job 5:17-18).

Spiritual wrestling matches are nothing new for Christians. It is through wrestling matches, dislocated hips, blood, and death that God gives his greatest blessings. We have the sure promise that we too can strive with God and prevail, because Jesus himself has overcome sin, death, and the devil through his own sacrificial death. His victory is ours, and we can take heart that even when God kills, he does so to make us live. Perhaps the battle of the *simul*, then, is not something to retreat from, but to courageously embrace.

The Unwelcome Surprise

There is a common myth that lurks on the fringes of our collective theological framework and does untold damage to the hearts and minds of many a sincere Christian. It is simply this: My moral capacity post-conversion should be drastically different from my moral capacity pre-conversion. The assumption seems to be that conversion effects such a seismic change in our moral capacities that we are

SINNER SAINT

fundamentally different beings. Conversion completely castrates our old sin nature, deadening the harmful urges that we once had. Or, at very least, it significantly lowers them, giving us the spiritual equivalent of a dose of Xanax. In short, the belief is that in Christians, the impulse to do good is now stronger than the impulse to do bad.

While there are places in Scripture we could go to respond to such a flawed notion (return to Chapter 2 for a sampling of such passages), perhaps the best approach would simply be to appeal to natural law by asking the question: Does such a view square with human experience? In other words, if we were to do a straw poll of Christians, would the majority say that doing good comes more naturally now than it did pre-conversion? All it takes is a cursory scan through church history to cast doubt on this widespread assumption. Whether it was justifying murder in the name of reclaiming the Holy Land throughout the Crusades, defending the American slave trade by cherry-picking Bible verses, or maintaining radio silence in the wake of the Nazi party's final solution to the "Jewish problem," the church has enough blots on her record to seriously question any such theory. In his commentary on Romans, New Testament scholar James Edwards makes this cutting observation: "It is saints, after all, not gangsters, who teach us the meaning of sin. The 'flesh' does not roll over dead at conversion; neither does it die easily thereafter. When threatened it fights for its life."[2]

---

[2] James R. Edwards, *Romans*, in "Understanding the Bible Commentary Series," edited by W. Ward Gasque, Robert L. Hubbard Jr., and Robert K. Johnson (Grand Rapids: Baker Books, 1992), 191.

EMBRACING THE BATTLE

For many Christians, this comes as a shock to our system. We thought that life with Jesus would be easier. We thought that worldly appeals would lose their luster. We thought that improvement would happen in leaps and bounds. Instead, some days feel like one step forward and two steps back. Progress is slow and plodding. Rather than running with perseverance the race marked out for us (Heb. 12:1), some days it seems like we're stuck on the sanctification treadmill. Forward movement is measured in inches rather than feet. Some of us never cease to be surprised when the battle with our inner sinner continues to wage fiercely no matter our age or life experience. We thought by now the enemy would have given up or at least slowed down. We thought there would be fewer bullets targeting us. We thought some sort of truce would have been reached. Yet still the war wages, and there we are in our foxhole: feeling under-resourced, outgunned, and exhausted. Is there any hope for the sinner-saint still engaged in hand-to-hand combat with their old sin nature?

Suiting Up

Ephesians 6 is a common go-to text among Christians seeking to give themselves a pep-talk before entering the fray of spiritual warfare. Here is the passage:

> Finally, be strong in the Lord and in the strength of his might. Put on the whole armor of God, that you may be able to stand against the schemes of the devil. For we do not wrestle against flesh and blood, but against the rulers, against the authorities, against the cosmic powers over this present

darkness, against the spiritual forces of evil in the heavenly places. Therefore take up the whole armor of God, that you may be able to withstand in the evil day, and having done all, to stand firm. Stand therefore, having fastened on the belt of truth, and having put on the breastplate of righteousness, and, as shoes for your feet, having put on the readiness given by the gospel of peace. In all circumstances take up the shield of faith, with which you can extinguish all the flaming darts of the evil one; and take the helmet of salvation, and the sword of the Spirit, which is the word of God, praying at all times in the Spirit, with all prayer and supplication. To that end, keep alert with all perseverance, making supplication for all the saints, and also for me, that words may be given to me in opening my mouth boldly to proclaim the mystery of the gospel, for which I am an ambassador in chains, that I may declare it boldly, as I ought to speak (Eph. 6:10-20).

I don't know about you, but these verses get my inner-*Braveheart* going, rallying me to fight the good fight. While such a reaction is not intrinsically wrong, if we dig a little deeper we'll find that the thrust of this passage points in another direction.

First off, who is doing the fighting in this spiritual battle? The obvious answer is: us. Christians. We are the ones picking up our weapons, fighting, shedding our blood, winning the war, etc. Onward Christian Soldiers, right? Yet if we zoom out and read this passage canonically, a different story emerges: the story of a God who fights the battles of his people. Caught between Pharaoh's army and the Red Sea, Moses sought to encourage the Israelites with these words: "Fear not, stand firm, and see the salvation of the Lord, which he will work for you today. For the Egyptians whom you see today, you shall never see again. The Lord will fight for you, and you have only to be silent" (Ex. 14:14). Who fights the battle? The Lord.

At the Cross, our Lord fought and overcame all the forces of sin which were too strong for us to defeat on our own. God saw us in our plight, stepped in, picked up a sword, and cut the head off the Serpent himself—all because he loves us. Ultimately, he fights the battle. He wins the war while we ride shotgun.

Notice also the weapons enumerated in this passage from Ephesians 6. Six pieces of equipment are listed: the belt of truth, the breastplate of righteousness, the shoes fitted in the readiness of the gospel, the shield of faith, the helmet of salvation, and the sword of the Spirit. Usually we look at these individually, assuming each should be treated in isolation from the others. Maybe one morning I forget to put on my belt of truth, so I am more susceptible to lies. Or possibly another day I forget to sharpen my sword of the Spirit (the Word of God) so I am less able to counter the enemy's blows. Yet if we take it as a truism that all Scripture is about Jesus (which Jesus himself makes clear; see Luke 24:25-27, 44-45) and that he is the lens that gives the right sense to any given text, other interpretive clues begin to emerge. The belt of truth, for example. Who is the way, *the truth*, and the life? Jesus (John 14:6 emphasis mine). What about the breastplate of righteousness and the helmet of salvation? Isaiah 59:17a tells us that "He [the Lord] put on righteousness as a breastplate, and a helmet of salvation on his head." In Aramaic, the name Jesus (Yehoshua) literally means "the Lord saves." Salvation, then, is Christologically-grounded. What about the feet fitted for the Gospel of peace? Who is the Prince of Peace? Again, Jesus (Isa. 9:6).

• 121 •

How about the sword of the Spirit, which is the Word of God? Who is the Word that became flesh and tabernacled among us? Jesus. If you are noticing a pattern here, you're on the right track. Commenting on the passage in the fourth and fifth centuries, early church father and Scripture translator, Jerome, makes the connection explicit: "It is one and the same thing to say 'put on the whole armor of God' and 'put on the Lord Jesus Christ.'"[3] Paul is telling us to armor up each and every day by being clothed in Christ. It's not about trying to remember each individual piece of equipment as soon as your head pops off the pillow each morning. Instead, he's saying that if you have Jesus, all of this is yours and more!

Paul writes this to the church in Colossae: "For in him [God's Son] all the fullness of God was pleased to dwell, and through him to reconcile to himself all things, whether on earth or in heaven, making peace by the blood of his cross" (Col. 1:19-20). As the old hymn goes, "Dressed in his righteousness alone, faultless to stand before the throne."[4] This means that, as we re-enter the fray of daily life, we do so secure in the knowledge that yesterday, today, and always, the battle truly is the Lord's.

At this point, we're finally ready to lay out a positive vision for Christian sanctification. What kind of progress is possible for the sinner-saint? What does growth look like? And what is our role in this? We'll touch on these questions and more in our final chapter.

---

[3] Jerome, *Epistle to the Ephesians* 3.6.11, quoted in Mark J. Edwards, *Galatians, Ephesians, Philippians*, ed. Thomas C. Oden, vol. 8, 36 vols., of *Ancient Christian Commentary on Scripture* (Downers Grove, Illinois: InterVarsity Press, 2006), 197.

[4] Edward Mote, "My Hope is Built on Nothing Less," 1834.

• 122 •

CHAPTER 10

Growing Down

THE OLDEST LIVING ORGANISM on earth is the Methuselah Tree, a bristlecone pine tree located in the remote Inyo National Forest in eastern California, somewhere in the White Mountains. The U.S. Forest Service keeps its precise location a secret in order to protect it from vandals. Bristlecone pines thrive in harsh environments where other trees cannot survive. They tend to grow just below the tree line in the high altitudes of mountainous regions where little healthy soil exists and they are exposed to the wind and elements. Due to these harsh conditions, they grow slowly and have a dense wood structure, making them more resistant than other trees to infestations of fungi and insects. From the surface up, bristlecones have a twisted, tortured look. The trunk and branches appear gnarled and deformed. It's almost like the tree is visibly grimacing. They're not especially tall, growing to a maximum height of forty or fifty feet. Their shallow, highly branched root system, however, can penetrate into underlying layers of rock such as limestone and dolomite to draw water, which is hard to come by in such extreme climates. Another unique feature about the roots is that they only feed the section of tree directly above them. The result is that bristlecones die in sections rather than all at once, allowing them to live longer. From the ground up, then, the Methuselah tree looks unimpressive. Some might even describe it as ugly. Yet its longevity lies in the unique root system, the downward growth that anchors it to the ground and keeps it supplied with nutrients. It is this which enables the tree to thrive.

The image of the Methuselah Tree is a helpful parallel to sanctification. When we speak of growth in the Christian life, usually we're envisioning impressive, upward growth, which is always visible and above the surface and can be observed with the naked eye. When oaks and roses and tomatoes grow, it is these parts which generally come to mind: trunks and branches and leaves and flowers and petals and stems and fruit and seeds and shoots. All of these grow upward. We can see them. Yet there is another element of growth that happens in a different direction, and that is downward. Beneath the surface, deep in the soil, in the blackened regions far from sunlight there is an unseen maturation process occurring. To the naked eye it is invisible, yet it is precisely this downward-thrusting root system that anchors the plant. In the same way, sanctification consists in growing deeper and deeper in our reliance upon Christ. Nowhere does the Bible describe growth in the life of the Christian as occurring apart from Christ. It is not a journey toward independence but dependence. It is growing down rather than growing up.

When we use the phrase "growing up," usually what we mean is the process by which someone comes to stand on his or her own two feet. They become able to manage their lives without the assistance of others. When a human moves through the stages of life from infant to baby to toddler to child to pre-teen to teenager to young adult, the goal is greater and greater independence with less and less reliance upon Mom and Dad. At some point they will be considered a grown-up, self-supporting and autonomous. For the Christian, however, self-reliance is not the goal. It is Christ-reliance we are after. Christian growth always happens in Christ rather than apart from him, which implies that sanctification is never a solo endeavor separated from our life in him. Rather, it occurs in close proximity to Jesus, the source of faith and life. Growing up implies leaving home behind. Growing down implies we never outgrow home because we never outgrow our need for Christ.

A brief survey of a number of New Testament passages will help clarify.

Biblical Metaphors

In John 15, Jesus has just finished washing his disciples' feet and is speaking to the twelve one final time prior to his passion. After promising the Holy Spirit and issuing words of peace and comfort, he says this:

> I am the vine, and my Father is the vinedresser. Every branch in me that does not bear fruit he takes away, and every branch that does bear fruit he prunes, that it may bear more fruit. Already you are clean because of the word I have spoken to you. Abide in me, and I in you. As the branch cannot bear fruit by itself, unless it abides in the vine, neither can you, unless you abide in me. I am the vine; you are the branches. Whoever abides in me and I in him, he it is that

bears much fruit, for apart from me you can do nothing (John 15:1-5).

In this word picture, Jesus speaks of himself as the vine while his father is the vinedresser. As disciples of Jesus, we are the branches whose ultimate goal is to bear fruit. So the vinedresser gets to work on us with his heavenly shears, pruning and cutting in an effort to establish a healthy tree. It is crucial to note, as has been mentioned earlier, that it is not the fruit which makes the tree. Verse three is key here: "*Already* you are clean because of the word that I have spoken to you" (emphasis mine). Believers in Jesus Christ have already been justified and cleansed by faith, declared righteous by God. The good works which follow do not make us righteous but rather serve as outward signs that we are righteous. The grapevine was already a grapevine before it produced any grapes. The production of grapes did not convert the plant from a "non-grapevine" into a grapevine. The vine was antecedent to the fruit.

Observe, too, the mechanism by which growth happens. The word "abide" is repeated over and over again in these verses. Believers are called to abide in Christ, the vine. Apart from him we cannot bear any fruit. In fact, we "can do nothing" (v. 5). The branches can only bear fruit if they are connected to the vine. The vine is the source of life, supplying nutrients to the branches, causing them to grow. The branches bear fruit only insofar as they are connected to the source of life. Growth apart from the vine is not just difficult; it is a sheer impossibility. Without that life-giving connection, all is lost and death results. The consequences are eternal: "If anyone does not abide in me he is thrown away like a branch and withers; and the branches are gathered, thrown into the fire, and burned" (v. 6). In light of this, it is important to notice that Jesus' command here is not to bear fruit, but to abide. For disciples, the focus is on maintaining that vital connection to Christ. The fruit is more of a byproduct rather than an end to be pursued in and of itself. Ultimately, this means that dependence, rather than independence, is the mark of a mature Christian.

Another verse commonly referenced regarding sanctification and Christian growth is Philippians 2:12: "Therefore, my beloved, as you have always obeyed, so now, not only in my presence but much more in my absence, work out your own salvation with fear and trembling." If any scriptural reference could be used to bolster the argument that sanctification is an independent, upward-trending solo endeavor, it would be this one. At first blush this text sounds like Paul is exhorting us to go it alone. We are to graduate from dependence to independence, developing the spiritual musculature to lift greater and greater loads as we work out our salvation. But the very next verse demonstrates the fallacy of such an understanding: "For it is God who works in you, both to will and to work for his good pleasure" (Phil. 2:13). Even the work we are tasked with is attributed to God alone. He is the source. Again, growth is never apart from the triune God but in connection to him. We grow down and deeper into him, not up and away from him.

In Romans 8, Paul speaks of the sanctifying work of the Holy Spirit, and he says this: "So then, brothers, we are debtors, not to the flesh, to live according to the flesh. For if you live according to the flesh you will die, but if by the Spirit you put to death the deeds of the body, you will live. For all who are led by the Spirit of God are sons of God" (Rom. 8:12-14). Paul says there are two different ways to live; by the flesh and by the Spirit. Living by the flesh means following our sinful desires and the temptations of the enemy, letting sin reign unchecked. Living by the Spirit, however, means being led in a new direction, fueled not by our own willpower but by the Holy Spirit. The verb for "put to death" in verse 13 is in the present tense, indicating that this won't be a once-and-done kind of thing. Instead, it is an ongoing task that will need to be repeated day after day. Such a fierce enemy cannot be slain by our own efforts but only by the power of the Spirit. In such a situation, growth translates to greater and greater reliance upon someone other than ourselves—namely, Christ, whom "the Spirit himself bears witness with our spirit that we are children of God, and if children, then heirs—heirs of God and fellow heirs with Christ" (vv. 16-17). For the Christian, Christless growth is not an option.

Finally, the author of Hebrews paints a vivid picture of one of the Bible's most famous (and misunderstood) metaphors regarding sanctification: "Therefore, since we are surrounded by so great a cloud of witnesses, let us also lay aside every weight, and sin which clings so closely, and let us run with endurance the race that is set before us" (Heb. 12:1). This is inspirational language with all the trappings of the victorious Christian life: a race, a crowd, a dramatic reversal, perseverance, and a singular decision to break with the old in favor of the new. You can picture the runner in your mind, pouring out her blood, sweat, and tears as she valiantly soldiers onward against all odds. On the home stretch now, she digs deep inside herself for the final push, throwing off the heavy garments of sin along the track as she successfully crosses the finish line through her own powers. Yet this inspiring interpretation does not line up with what we read in the very next verse: "looking to Jesus, the founder and perfecter of our faith, who for the joy that was set before him endured the cross, despising the shame and is seated at the right hand of the throne of God" (v. 2). The only one who ran the race set out for him faithfully to the end was Jesus. He succeeds where we fail. Where the first Adam gave in to the temptations of Satan, Jesus went toe-to-toe with the devil and defeated him. Where Israel grumbled and complained about their lack of leeks and lamb, Jesus sacrificed his own body on the tree to become the bread of life for the whole world. Where we tend to bow down to the gods around us and within us, Jesus worships his heavenly father alone. Where we are faithless, he remains faithful, enduring the cross for the joy set before him so that all who believe might have eternal life. Not only does the author of Hebrews describe Jesus as the founder of our faith; he is also the perfecter of our faith. He not only starts us out on our spiritual journey, but he sees us through. He brings our faith to completion, justifying and sanctifying us. It is not being perfect but relying on the one who is perfect that is of ultimate importance in the Christian life.

Progress: Returning to the Scene of the Crime

In light of this, the question naturally arises about whether we can speak of progress in the Christian life. Is such a term appropriate and, if so, in what sense? If we understand sanctification as growing down (deeper in Christ) rather than growing up (in autonomy), what does progress even mean? And how do we quantify it? Can progress be marked in the same way we measure a child's growth, with pencil marks on the wall? Are there appropriate metrics we might utilize to determine whether someone is getting better?

Part of the way we respond to that question is dependent upon how seriously we take sin. Theologian Oswald Bayer makes this helpful clarification:

> The guilt of sin… is… no mere tinder, but rather a brightly blazing flame. It is truly and completely sin; sin qualifies humans in their entirety. Therefore sin is to be understood qualitatively not quantitatively. There are no fractions when it comes to sin. The same is true of faith; it is whole (totus) and without fractions.[1]

Being a *simul* means we are—contrary to all mathematical laws—one hundred percent sinner and one hundred percent saint. We don't deal in fractions or decimal places. The category "sinner" is a qualitative rather than a quantitative identity marker, which means that any attempt to measure the stature of our inner sinner or inner saint is misguided from the start. God's verdict is either guilty or innocent. Those are the only two options. James makes this clear when he tells us that "whoever keeps the whole law but fails in one point has become guilty of all of it" (James 2:10). So when we use terms like "less" or "more" to evaluate our progress against particular sins, we're failing to take into account the all-encompassing nature of our

---

[1] Oswald Bayer, "Luther's Simul Iustus et Peccator," in *Simul: Inquiries into Luther's Experience of the Christian Life*, ed. Robert Kolb, Torbjörn Johansson, and Daniel Johansson (Gottingen: Vandenhoeck & Ruprecht, 2021), 44.

identities as sinner-saints. We're overestimating the power of sin and underestimating the power of the Cross.

If we use the word "progress" to describe the Christian life, perhaps the best we can do is to say we daily begin again.[2] We daily return to our starting point. This isn't as fatalistic as it sounds. Christians never grow beyond their need for Jesus. We are called instead to start every day at the foot of the cross, confessing our own dire need for a Savior. Rather than insisting upon progress as a precondition for God's love, we ground our identity in his merciful and gracious character. He is a long-suffering father who never stops loving his wayward children. Sinner-saints regard the parable of the prodigal son not simply as a picture of conversion but an accurate portrayal of our daily struggles. Every moment we stand in need of the unconditional love of a gracious heavenly father who moves first, who sees us from a long way off and runs to embrace us and forgive us, reinstating us as his children and bringing us to repentance. This is where sinner-saints start. From such a posture, we can rise confidently to face the fray of the world, the flesh, and the devil, fighting fiercely against their mastery. We claim the truth that we are no longer servants of sin but servants of righteousness, and that sin is no longer lord over us. God daily renews his image in us, enabling us to fight against sin.

This side of heaven, of course, sanctification will always remain incomplete. Despite what the army recruiters may promise, we'll never be all we can be. Yet such a reality need not discourage us. Instead, it saves us from the crushing weight of perfectionism by grounding our

---

[2] This language of "beginning again" is adapted from Luther, especially his lectures on Romans.

selfhood firmly and securely in Christ. He is our all in all. So we return to him, again and again, the author and perfecter of our faith. As astounding as it may seem, we can even return to the scene of the crime, however grisly it may be, knowing that his blood is sufficient to cover our sin. I know what you're thinking! And the answer is Yes, even *that* sin.

New Birth

There is one last piece to this theological puzzle that we've glossed over up to this point, and that is the doctrine of regeneration, sometimes referred to as the new birth.[3] Whenever we focus on a particular doctrine, we inherently run the risk of de-emphasizing others or, at very least, relegating them to the sidelines. Unfortunately, this necessary evil is simply a part of the theological enterprise. For example, when we make much of eschatology, the whole "loving thy neighbor" business in the here-and-now of earthly existence can be devalued. Or when we highlight the centrality of faith, the accusation automatically follows, "Yeah, but what about works?" The same principle holds true in our present discussion of sinner-saints. We've focused much on the forensic doctrine of justification and how God declares us righteous not because of our own merits but solely on the basis of Christ. He forgives us for Christ's sake, and declares us innocent. However, God's work doesn't end with a declaration, nor

---

[3] For a helpful explanation of how the doctrine of regeneration disappeared during the Lutheran orthodox period, see Paul Hinlicky's talk, "How the Holy Spirit Disappeared from Lutheranism," delivered during the Braaten-Benne lectures of 2019 (https://www.podbean.com/ew/pb-ia43b-c3de9f). His overall argument is that the Formula of Concord's heavy use of forensic language downplayed an earlier emphasis on regeneration in the Apology to the Augsburg Confession.

is his work exclusively limited to the courtroom. Instead, he reveals his truth in a plethora of ways, like facets of a diamond, and one of those facets is regeneration.

In Jesus' conversation with Nicodemus, he spells out this teaching with crystal clarity:

> Jesus replied, "Very truly I tell you, no one can see the kingdom of God unless they are born again." "How can someone be born when they are old?" Nicodemus asked. "Surely they cannot enter a second time into their mother's womb to be born!" Jesus answered, "Very truly I tell you, no one can enter the kingdom of God unless they are born of water and the Spirit. Flesh gives birth to flesh, but the Spirit gives birth to spirit. You should not be surprised at my saying, 'You must be born again.' The wind blows wherever it pleases. You hear its sound, but you cannot tell where it comes from or where it is going. So it is with everyone born of the Spirit" (John 3:3-8).

Other key passages include 2 Corinthians 5:17, John 1:12-13, and Ephesians 4:22-24. The idea here is that God is doing something new in the life of the believer. He is bringing a new creation into being. In one sense, that new being is already here. Yet in another sense, it is not fully realized. As paradoxical as it may sound, we are becoming who we already are in Christ. We are new creations, spiritually reborn in the same way that a newborn baby is brought into this world. God regenerates us, transforming us and changing our desires so that we love God, love others, and even seek to do his will. We are transformed, not simply in a declarative sense but in an actualized sense. We are not saints in theory but in practice, whose hearts and minds are really being renewed in the image of Christ and whose behavior reflects that change. The Holy Spirit daily empowers us to fight against our inner sinner, freeing us from its tyrannical power and enabling us to live differently. He truly enlightens, enlivens, and sanctifies us. As Thomas Oden puts it: "Christ died to deliver us not only from the guilt of sin but from the power of sin."[4]

The doctrine of the new birth reminds us that God is not a calculator. His ultimate concern is not with balance sheets or whether the accounts are in the red or black. His real love is not for numbers but for people. What bothers him most is not that the scales are unbalanced but that lost sinners are dying apart from him, and the only thing that can save them is the person and work of Jesus Christ! He is not Ebenezer Scrooge, crying "humbug" with every misplaced decimal. He cares about people. He has compassion on them and actively yearns for their salvation. He is not cold and uncaring but deeply moved by our sorry state of affairs. He was so moved, in fact, that he sent his one and only Son into the world, that whoever believes in him should have eternal life (John 3:16). The scales must certainly be balanced. Jesus' righteousness must be reckoned to our account and our sin imputed to his. Through faith, we are now in the black. Yet in the end, all this account-balancing is penultimate in the sense that even this is in service to the salvation of souls. God doesn't love spreadsheets. He loves you!

Ultimately, the new birth puts flesh on the theological bones of imputation and forensic justification. Doctrine alone is not alive and

---

[4] Thomas C. Oden, *Classic Christianity* (San Francisco: HarperCollins, 2009), 659.

active. People, however, are. While truth itself is objective, life is lived subjectively, and the new birth gives us language to speak of this. The new birth takes the *simul* out of the ether and grounds it in real life, insisting that God is not only a divine judge but a friend of sinners. It takes us out of the lecture hall and chalkboard and into the world with its teeming masses of human beings with all of their multifaceted complexities. He wants to rectify not just our status, but our relationship with him. In other words, in the depths of God's heart is not simply a concern about a verdict but a desire for reconciliation with his lost creation. His goal is not merely a changed status but a fundamentally transformed relationship.

Pastoral Implications

Ok. It's time to get specific. Let's bring this whole theological discussion of the *simul* down to earth. Enough Latin terms. Enough highfalutin book learnin'. Enough Luther and Augustine. Let's talk brass tacks. How does affirming that humans are sinner-saints actually translate to real life people facing real-life struggles? How would you counsel someone struggling with, say, an anger problem, differently from than a counselor who held a more optimistic view of human nature? If someone walked into your office at church, plopped down in a chair, and began to bare their soul about the depths of their sin, what difference would holding to a sinner-saint paradigm make? How would it affect the way you saw them and treated them? How might you pastor someone differently?

Let's do a case study. I offer this example not to show what an ideal pastor would do. I am not an ideal pastor. I have never met an ideal pastor, mostly because they don't exist. (If you ever meet one, run the other way.) I offer this scenario simply as a starting point for further discussion. I believe there are many helpful tactics one could take and words one could offer in such a situation. The following example is only meant to illuminate how a realistic appraisal of human nature might affect the way we treat others, including the advice we so readily offer.

Joe has anger issues, and he knows it. He's struggled since before he can remember. In high school his anger reared its head every now and again, especially on the football field. When calls didn't go his way, he'd secretly grind his cleats into his opponents' hands at the bottom of the fumble pile. Sometimes the anger manifested as an outburst in an argument with family. He'd pray about it, repent, eventually apologize, and go on with his life. But now he's thirty-one years old with a family of his own: a wife and a young child. The pressure of increasing work demands combined with the sleepless nights of new parenthood have created a perfect storm of emotions. Miles away from friends and family and with no friends he feels he can talk to, he's been lashing out at his wife. He turns her into the enemy, making her the object of his wrath. It hurts. It hurts her, it hurts him, it hurts their marriage, and it hurts their young child who has a front row seat to these heated exchanges. It's not good, and he knows something has to change or his family will end up in ruins. One Sunday after church, he marches into my office at his wits' end. Barely has the door closed when he blurts out his confession in its entirety. As you look into his eyes, you see a mixture of equal parts frustration, fear, exhaustion, confusion, and sadness: "Pastor, what should I do?!"

My first move, once I've resisted (to the best of my ability) absorbing the anxiety Joe is emanating, is to recognize the mechanics behind his question. On the surface, he's asking for advice. "What should I do?" demands an answer in terms of practical steps he can take to overcome his anger. Yet it is precisely at this point that I need to squelch my impulse to be the "life advice giver"—as attractive as this might be for my wizened, thirty-eight-year-old ego. Our knee-jerk response when someone comes to us with a problem is to start throwing down life advice. "Well, have you tried this? What about that? Here's another strategy you might want to employ." These are words of law; DO and DO NOT. More law will fix the situation, or so we think. But in my haste to draw my law pistol to shoot Joe down, I fail to recognize the possibility that he may already be dead. The law is doing its killing work on him even as we speak, as he experiences the consequences his sinful actions are wreaking on his own family. He's feeling it. He's in the midst of it. I've known Joe for years and can see it in his face. Joe needs the gospel. So instead of doling out life advice, I begin by reminding him of his identity in Christ. He is a baptized child of God. He is someone for whom Jesus died. He is beloved and fully forgiven. There is no condemnation for those who are in Christ Jesus (Rom. 8:1), I tell him, and God has cast his sin as far as the east is from the west (Ps. 103:12). The devil is trying to tempt Joe to believe the lie that he is nothing more than his mistakes. My task in that moment is to remind him of a deeper, truer reality: He is God's child, and God's love is not contingent on his performance but is secure through faith in Christ. That is the biggest truth he has forgotten. Satan is tempting him to despair, and he needs the good news of the gospel to unburden him from the crushing weight of the law. This needs to be the starting point.

From here, the conversation turns toward behavior. Specifically, anger and its killing power (Matt. 5:21-22). In his own words, he sees red and he's powerless to stop himself, plain and simple. I raise the question, "Right, but is that actually true? Is it actually true that you are powerless to stop your anger?" From there we talk about our new identities in Christ, and how God sends the Holy Spirit to help us fight against such destructive passions. We serve a new master and Lord, who calls us to live differently. He pushes back, "Right, but I CAN'T live differently pastor! I try and I pray and I try again and I pray again and I apologize again, but it's not getting any better!" We speak about the fruit of the Spirit and how God's promise of growth never has the word "quantifiable" attached to it. It is a slow process. I tell him that he's right; he can't! And that's why he needs Jesus. "That sounds too easy, Pastor," he says. "So what, then? Am I fated to sin? Am I destined to keep failing and failing the rest of my life? Shouldn't I be getting better? Isn't that what sanctification is all about? Progress?! Improvement?!" As ironic as it sounds, I tell him, the fact that he's experiencing such angst is actually a good thing. It's a sign of life, that the Holy Spirit is at work within him, killing his old Adam and making him a new creation. The real danger would be if he didn't see his anger as a problem. We talk more. Mostly I just listen. I mention an "Emotions Anonymous" group that meets in the area. He's not sure but agrees to check it out. We discuss the possibility of him meeting with a mentor friend to talk and pray for the next few months. I ask him to close in prayer. He prays for God to help him manage his anger, for an attitude of repentance and forgiveness, and for God to heal the wounds in his family. Just like they teach every good pastor to do in seminary, I end our conversation with a C.S. Lewis quote. There are hugs all around. The course of his life is forever altered, he and his family live happily ever after, and the pastor gets a raise. (OK, now I'm just being ridiculous.)

There is no quick fix. There is no silver bullet. But there is always hope for actual change—for Joe and for you—because of Jesus, and the sure promise that his grace is greater than our sin. Such truth makes an infinite difference in the lives of sinner-saints. It means that God loves us, but it also means that he loves us too much to allow us to remain in our sin.

Into the Crevasse

Progress in the Christian life looks less like growing up and more like growing down. The life of the Christian looks less like ascending toward the peak of perfect sanctification and more like a downward traverse into the crevasse of Jesus' all-sufficiency.

In her book, *The Vulnerable Pastor*, author Mindy Smith tells the story of mountaineer Joe Simpson's scrape with death. This story provides a poignant metaphor for sanctification:

Thousands of feet up the side of the Siula Grande mountain, Joe's safety line was cut, leaving Joe to slide with a broken leg into a deep crevasse. After several desperate attempts to climb up and out of the crevasse, he was faced with the fact that his injury made it impossible. And so, against all survival instinct, he made the excruciating choice to lower himself deeper into the crevasse in the hope that there would be other exits farther down, all the time wondering, *Am I lowering myself to freedom or deeper into the belly of the earth? Does a ray of sunlight await me in the pit, showing a way out into day, or is there only darkness and slow death?* With every inch he lowered himself down, he edged farther from the obvious way to life—and there was no way back up.[5]

Ultimately, Joe's decision was the right one, as he was able to make his way to safety and rescue.

For Christians, the way down is the way up. It is counterintuitive. It is against all survival instincts. And yet it is the way of Jesus:

> Very truly I tell you, unless a kernel of wheat falls to the ground and dies, it remains only a single seed. But if it dies, it produces many seeds. Anyone who loves their life will lose it, while anyone who hates their life in this world will keep it for eternal life (John 12:24-25).

Christ lived by dying. He became first by making himself last. He did not do his own will but instead did the will of his heavenly father. In the same way, the call for Christians is to crucify our own desires and ambitions so that we might live for God and our neighbor. It is down, through the crevasse, that we summit the peak of the Christian life.

Death is the great leveler. As the great theologian Aaron Burr has taught us: "Death doesn't discriminate between the sinners and the

---

[5] Mandy Smith, *The Vulnerable Pastor* (Downers Grove: InterVarsity Press, 2015), 52-53.

saints. It takes and it takes and it takes."[6] Whether you've defeated your gambling addiction completely or keep falling off the wagon and seem to return to square one, death doesn't care. You are going to die one day. That is not pessimism but realism talking. In the grand scheme of God's redemptive plans, earthly sanctification is not at the center. This is not to say that the doctrine doesn't matter. It is only to say that progress in the Christian life is not the cause of salvation. Rather, it is the result of it. Downward in Christ, rather than upward in self-sufficiency, must be our battle cry.

As Martin Luther so succinctly put it:

This life is not righteousness, but growth in righteousness; not health, but healing; not being, but becoming; not rest, but exercise. We are not yet what we shall be, but we are growing toward it; the process is not yet finished, but it is going on; this is not the end, but it is the road; all does not yet gleam with glory, but all is being purified.[7]

---

[6] Lin-Manuel Miranda, "Wait For It," track 13 on *Hamilton* (Original Broadway Cast Recording), Atlantic Recording, 2015, compact disc.

[7] Martin Luther, *Defense and Explanation of All the Articles*, quoted in "Rethinking Luther, Rethinking Myself," by Joey Goodall, Mockingbird, April 21, 2021, https://mbird.com/literature/rethinking-luther-rethinking-myself/.

CHAPTER 11

Jesus,
Friend of Saints

IN CHAPTER 1, I told two stories, both true. The first involved my own personal struggles with sanctification throughout life, wrestling with how to answer the perpetual question, "Why am I not better than I am?" The second involved a pastoral visit I had with an elderly couple, the husband tearfully expressing both remorse and confusion at his own actions: "I know exactly what it is I'm supposed to do, pastor! So why the hell don't I do it?!" Let's revisit those stories.

In story number one, during the heat of one of my most intense sanctification battles, I mentioned that I decided to phone a mentor friend of mine to vent my frustrations. I intentionally omitted his response, but I want to share it with you now. I asked him, point blank, why I, as a lifelong Christian, still wrestled so mightily with sin. Shouldn't it be less of a struggle at this point? Shouldn't I have some measurable progress to show? He was an older, wiser pastor who had spent years in the trenches. He knew what I was going through, and he knew what I needed to hear. He told me, "I hear you, Luke. But you know, the older I get and the more intimately I become acquainted with my own sin, the more I realize how much I need Jesus."

In the second story, as I entered the apartment of this elderly couple in a memory unit of a small nursing home and assessed the aftermath of the heated exchange between this husband and wife of sixty-seven years, I was at a loss for words. Luckily, the husband found them for me. He said, "You know marriage really makes you realize things about yourself. It makes me realize how sinful I am; how weak I am. The only thing I can think to do in these circumstances is to rely upon God. I mean, what else can I do?" In his own way, he was coming to grips with the reality of the sinner-saint. Yet he knew that this situation wasn't hopeless. He knew that his only hope was his Lord and Savior. As Dr. Rod Rosenbladt so memorably put it, he was betting all the blue chips on Jesus and his blood alone.

The goal of this book has been to show—not just with a theological but a pastoral eye—that the *simul* is the normative experience for the Christian life. We are at the same time saints and sinners, at once righteous and sinful, not partially but fully. Ironically, such a confession leads not to despair as one might imagine but to true freedom. It frees us from the exhausting task of trying to prove we are better than we are or, at the very least, better than the person next to us. It frees us from the untenable weight of unrealistic expectations, both our own and others. It frees us to love people not as we would have them but as they actually are. It frees us from constantly having to live up to some standard of "enoughness,"[1] whether in the

---

[1] This term is borrowed from David Zahl. For a more thorough explanation of the topic, check out his book *Seculosity* (Minneapolis: Augsburg Fortress, 2019).

realm of parenting, academics, professionally, etc. It frees us from the need for virtue signaling, because our own inherent goodness is not the measure of our worth. It frees us from having to downplay the law to make it more do-able because it is now fulfilled in Christ. It frees us from soft-pedaling sin by maintaining the depths of our depravity and the strength of our Savior. It frees us from the tyranny of legalism by insisting we are not judged on the basis of obedience but on the basis of faith alone. It frees us from the endless treadmill of life, where there is always more to do, by telling us "It is finished!" Our new identity now rests not on what we do (good or bad), but on what Jesus has done for us.

As we learned earlier, the moment we cease to be a *simul* is the moment we cease to need Jesus. To be sure, it is a temporary identity, as one day soon he will return to take us to be forever with the Lord, where there will be no more sin. He will purge the sinner and only the saint will remain. Yet the *simul* is an identity we need not be ashamed of because Jesus has already borne all of our sorrows and shame on the tree. We can wear the "sinner-saint" label fully, joyfully embracing the reality that though we may be great sinners, we have an even greater Savior. God does not turn us away because of who we are. Instead, he is ever our friend—welcoming us, healing us, and inviting us back home.

Acknowledgements

I WANT TO EXPRESS a deep gratitude to the churches who graciously allowed me to serve as their pastor: Stavanger Lutheran Church, Bunker Hill Lutheran Brethren Church, and Elim Lutheran Church. As a young shepherd-in-training, this book would not have been possible without your patience, forgiveness, and encouragement as I've clumsily learned to maneuver the rod and staff of my craft.

To my wife, who selflessly shouldered the burden of childrearing to make space for this project and who continues to model grace in ways I find equally humbling and astounding. She also served as a constant conversation partner in the writing of this book, shedding light on blind spots and sharpening my thinking.

To my girls, Marigold and Liliana: Your Dad loves you so much! Thank you for the gift of being your father and for loving me when I was at my most unlovable. I wish there were more pictures in this book for you to enjoy.

To my mom and dad, who always encouraged my writing efforts.

To Scott Keith, Dan Price, Seth Moorman, and everyone at 1517 for proposing this project in the first place and for believing in my voice, even when I had my doubts. Steve Byrnes and Sam Leanza Ortiz, in publishing, for their tireless encouragement and guidance. Special thanks go out to Kelsi Klembara, editor extraordinaire, for load-testing every phrase to see if it would bear weight. If there is anything original in this book, it is likely due to her insight.

Finally, a big shout out to Common Grounds Coffee House in Alexandria & Jitters Java Cafe in Sauk Centre, Minnesota, for providing the atmosphere and caffeinated fuel I needed to power through the long hours of writing.

Soli Deo Gloria.

More Best Sellers from

Find these titles
and more at 1517.org/shop

Explore daily articles, podcasts, videos, and more.

Visit **www.1517.org**
for free Gospel resources.